THINK
& GROW
RICH!

THINK & GROW RICH!

NAPOLEON HILL

Pacific Publishing Studio

ISBN is 1453670114

EAN-13 is 9781453670118

To order a copy of this book,

Special acknowledgement is made to the following:
Transcription: Pacific Publishing Studio

Think and Grow Rich

TRIBUTES TO THE AUTHOR

From Great American Leaders

THINK AND GROW RICH was 25 years in the making. It is Napoleon Hill's most popular book, based on his famous Law of Success Philosophy. His work and writings have been praised by great leaders in finance, education, politics, government.

Supreme Court of the United States
Washington, D. C.

Dear Mr. Hill,

I have now had an opportunity to finish reading your Law of Success textbooks and I wish to express my appreciation of the splendid work you have done in the organization of this philosophy.

It would be helpful if every politician in the country would assimilate and apply the principles upon which your lessons are based. It contains some very fine material, which every leader in every walk of life should understand.

I am happy to have had the privilege of rendering you some slight measure of help in the organization of this splendid course of "common sense" philosophy.

Sincerely yours

(President and former Chief Justice of the United States, Howard Taft)

"By applying many of the fundamentals of the Law of Success philosophy, we have built a great chain of successful stores. I presume it would be no exaggeration of fact if I said that the Woolworth Building might properly be called a monument to the soundness of these principles." *F. W. WOOLWORTH*

"I feel greatly indebted for the privilege of reading your book. If I had had this philosophy fifty years ago, I suppose I could have accomplished all that I have done in less than half the time. I sincerely hope the world will discover and reward you." *ROBERT DOLLAR*

"Mastery of the Law of Success philosophy is the equivalent of an insurance policy against failure." *SAMUEL GOMPERS*

"May I not congratulate you on your persistence. Any man who devotes that much time . . . must of necessity make discoveries of great value to others. I am deeply impressed by your interpretation of the 'Master Mind' principles which you have so clearly described." *WOODROW WILSON*

"I know that your fundamentals of success are sound because I have been applying them in my business for more than thirty years." *JOHN WANAMAKER*

"I know that you are doing a world of good with your Law of Success. I would not care to set a monetary value on this training because it brings to the student qualities which cannot be measured by money alone." *GEORGE EASTMAN (Eastman Kodak)*

"Whatever success I may have attained I owe, entirely, to the application of your fundamental principles of the Law of Success. I believe I have the honor of being your first student." *W.M. WRIGLEY, JR.*

Contents

AUTHOR'S PREFACE

EVERY CHAPTER OF this book mentions the money-making secret that has made fortunes for more than five hundred exceedingly wealthy people, whom I have carefully analyzed over a period of years. The secret was brought to my attention by Andrew Carnegie, more than a quarter of a century ago. The canny, lovable old Scotsman carelessly tossed it into my mind, when I was but a boy. Then he sat back in his chair, with a merry twinkle in his eyes, and watched carefully to see if I had brains enough to understand the full significance of what he had said to me.

When he saw that I had grasped the idea, he asked if I would be willing to spend twenty years or more, preparing myself to take it to the world, to men and women who, without the secret, might go through life as failures. I said I would, and with Mr. Carnegie's cooperation, I have kept my promise. This book contains that secret, after having been put to a practical test by thousands of people, in almost every walk of life. It was Mr. Carnegie's idea that the magic formula, which gave him a stupendous fortune, ought to be placed within reach of people who do not have time to investigate how people make money. It was his hope that I might test and demonstrate the soundness of the formula through the experience of men and women in every calling. He believed the formula should be taught in all public schools and colleges. He believed that, if properly taught, it could revolutionize the educational system so that the time spent in school could be reduced to less than half.

His experience with Charles M. Schwab, and other young men of Mr. Schwab's type, convinced Mr. Carnegie that much of that which is taught in the schools is of no value in the business of earning a living or accumulating riches. He had arrived at this decision, because he had taken into his business one young man after another, many of them with very little schooling, and by coaching them in the use of this formula, developed in them rare leadership. Moreover, *his coaching made fortunes for everyone who followed his instructions.*

In the chapter on Faith, you will read the astounding story of the organization of the giant United States Steel Corporation, as it was conceived and carried out by one of the young men through whom Mr. Carnegie proved that his formula works *for all who are ready for it.* This single application of the secret, by that young man, Charles M. Schwab, made him a huge fortune in both money and OPPORTUNITY. Roughly speaking, this particular application of the formula was worth *six hundred million dollars.* These facts—and they are facts well known to almost everyone who knew Mr. Carnegie—give you a fair idea of what the reading of this book may bring to you, provided that you *KNOW WHAT YOU WANT.*

Even before it had undergone twenty years of practical testing, the secret was passed on to more than one hundred thousand people who have used it for their personal benefit.. Some have made fortunes with it. Others have used it successfully in creating harmony in their homes. A clergyman used it so effectively that it brought him an income of upwards of $75,000.00 a year. Arthur Nash, a Cincinnati tailor, used his near-bankrupt business as a "guinea pig" on which to test the formula. The business came to life and made a fortune for its owners. It is still thriving, although Mr. Nash has gone. The experiment was so unique that newspapers and magazines gave it more than a million dollars' worth of positive publicity.

The secret was passed on to Stuart Austin Wier, of Dallas, Texas. He was ready for it—so ready that he gave up his profession and studied law. Did he succeed? That story is told too. I gave the secret to Jennings Randolph the day he graduated from college, and he used it so successfully that he served fourteen years in the U.S. House of Representatives and twenty-six in the Senate, where he authored the constitutional amendment that gave eighteen year olds the right to vote. While serving as advertising manager of the LaSalle Extension University, when it was little more than a name, I had the privilege of seeing J. G. Chapline, President of the University, use the formula so effectively that he has since made the LaSalle one of the great extension schools of the country.

The secret to which I refer is mentioned no fewer than a hundred times, throughout this book. It has not been directly named, for it seems to work more successfully when it is merely uncovered and left in sight, where THOSE WHO ARE READY and SEARCHING FOR IT may pick it up. That is why Mr. Carnegie tossed it to me so quietly, without giving me its specific name. If you are READY to put it to use, you will recognize this secret at least once in every chapter. I wish I might feel privileged to tell you how you will know if you are ready, but that would deprive you of much of the benefit you will receive when you make the discovery in your own way.

While this book was being written, my son, who was then finishing his last year of college, picked up the manuscript of chapter two, read it, and discovered the secret for himself. He used the information so effectively that he went directly into a responsible position at a beginning salary greater than the average person ever earns. His story has been briefly described in chapter two. When you read it, perhaps you will dismiss any feeling you may have had, at the beginning of the book, that it promised too much. Additionally, if you have ever been discouraged, if you have had difficulties to surmount which took the very soul out of you, if you have tried and failed, if you were ever handicapped by illness or physical affliction, this story of my son's discovery and use of the Carnegie formula may prove to be your oasis in the Desert of Lost Hope.

This secret was extensively used by President Woodrow Wilson during the World War. It was passed on to every soldier who fought in the war, carefully wrapped in the training received before going to the front. President Wilson told me it was a strong factor in raising the funds needed for the war. More than twenty years ago, Hon. Manuel L. Quezon (then Resident Commissioner of the Philippine Islands), was inspired by the secret to gain freedom for his people. He gained freedom for the Philippines, and was the first President of the free state.

A peculiar thing about this secret is that those who acquire it and use it find themselves literally swept into success with very little effort, and they never again submit to failure! If you doubt this, study the names of those who have used it, wherever they have been mentioned; check their records for yourself and be convinced.

There is no such thing as SOMETHING FOR NOTHING! The secret to which I refer cannot be had without a price, although the price is far less than its value. It cannot be had at any price by those who are not intentionally searching for it. It cannot be given away, it cannot be purchased for money. The secret serves equally well, all who are ready for it. Education has nothing to do with it. Long before I was born, the secret had found its way to Thomas A. Edison, and he used it so intelligently that he became the world's leading inventor, even though he had only three months of schooling. The secret was passed on to a business associate of Mr. Edison. He used it so effectively that he went from making $12,000 a year to amassing a fortune and retiring young. You will find his story at the beginning of the first chapter. It should convince you that riches are not beyond your reach, that you can still be what you want to be, that money, fame, recognition, and happiness can be had by all who are ready and determined to have them.

How do I know these things? You should have the answer before you finish this book. You may find it in the very first chapter or on the last page. While I was performing the twenty year task of research, which I had undertaken at Mr. Carnegie's request, I analyzed hundreds of well known people, many of whom admitted that they had accumulated their vast fortunes through the aid of the Carnegie secret; among these men were:

HENRY FORD	ARTHUR BRISBANE
WILLIAM WRIGLEY JR.	WOODROW WILSON
JOHN WANAMAKER	W.M. HOWARD TAFT
JAMES J. HILL	LUTHER BURBANK
GEORGE S. PARKER	EDWARD W. BOK
E. M. STATLER	FRANK A. MUSEY
HENRY L. DOHERTY	ELBERT H. GARY
CYRUS H. K. CURTIS	ALEXANDER GRAHAM
GEORGE EASTMAN	BELL
CHARLES M. SCHWAB	JOHN H. PATTERSON
HARRIS F. WILLIAMS	JULIUS ROSENWALD
DR. FRANK GUNSAULUS	STUART AUSTIN WIER
WILLIAM JENNINGS BRYAN	THEODORE ROOSEVELT
FRANK CRANE	DANIEL WILLARD
KING GILLETTE	GEORGE M. ALEXANDER
RALPH A. WEEKS	J.G. CHAPLINE
JUDGE DANIEL T. WRIGHT	JENNINGS RANDOLPH
JOHN D. ROCKEFELLER	ARTHUR NASH
THOMAS A. EDISON	CLARENCE DARROW
FRANK A. VANDERLIP	J. ODGEN ARMOUR
F. W. WOOLWORTH	DR. DAVID S. JORDAN
COL. ROBERT A. DOLLAR	WILBUR WRIGHT
EDWARD A. FILENE	ELBERT HUBBARD
EDWIN C. BARNES	JOHN W. DAVIS

These names represent only a small fraction of the hundreds of well known Americans whose achievements, financially and otherwise, prove that those who understand and apply the Carnegie secret reach high stations in life. I have never known anyone who was inspired to use the secret, who did not achieve noteworthy success, and I have never known anyone to distinguish themselves, or to accumulate riches of any consequence, without possession of the secret. From these two facts, I draw the conclusion that the secret is more important, as a part of the knowledge essential for self-determination, than any other level of education. What is EDUCATION, anyway? This has been answered in full detail.

As far as schooling is concerned, many of these people had very little. John Wanamaker once told me that what little schooling he had, he acquired in very much the same manner as a modern locomotive takes on water, by "scooping it up as it runs." Henry Ford never reached high school, let alone college. I am not attempting to minimize the value of education, but I am trying to express my earnest belief that those who master and apply the secret will reach high stations, accumulate riches, and bargain with life on their own terms, even if their education has been limited.

Somewhere, as you read, the secret to which I refer will jump from the page and stand boldly before you, IF YOU ARE READY FOR IT! When it appears, you will recognize it. Whether you receive the sign in the first or the last chapter, stop for a moment when it presents itself, and turn down a glass, for that occasion will mark the most important turning-point of your life.

We pass now, to Chapter One, and to the story of my very dear friend, who has generously acknowledged having seen the mystic sign, and whose business achievements are evidence enough that he turned down a glass. As you read his story, as well as the others, remember that they deal with the important problems of life that we all experience. The problems arising from one's quest to earn a living, to find hope, courage, contentment, and peace of mind; to accumulate riches and to enjoy the freedoms it affords.

Remember, too, as you go through the book, that it deals with facts and not with fiction, its purpose being to convey a great universal truth through which all who are READY may learn, not only WHAT TO DO, BUT ALSO HOW TO DO IT and will receive, as well, THE MOTIVATION TO START.

Before you begin the first chapter, I'd like to offer one brief suggestion which may provide a clue by which the Carnegie secret may be recognized. It is this: *ALL ACHIEVEMENT, ALL EARNED RICHES, HAVE THEIR BEGINNING IN AN IDEA!* If you are ready for the secret, you already possess half of it, therefore, you will readily recognize the other half the moment it reaches your mind.

Napoleon Hill

INTRODUCTION

THE MAN WHO "THOUGHT" HIS WAY INTO PARTNERSHIP WITH THOMAS A. EDISON

TRULY, THOUGHTS ARE things. They become powerful things when they are mixed with definite purpose, persistence, and a BURNING DESIRE for their translation into riches or other material objects. A little more than thirty years ago, Edwin C. Barnes discovered how true it is that people really do THINK AND GROW RICH. His discovery did not come about suddenly. It came little by little, beginning with a BURNING DESIRE to become a business partner of the great Thomas Edison. One of the chief characteristics of Barnes' DESIRE was that it was *definite*. He wanted to work *with* Edison, not *for* him. Pay close attention to *how* he went about translating his DESIRE into reality, and you will have a better understanding of the thirteen principles that lead to riches.

When this DESIRE, or impulse of thought, first flashed into his mind, he was in no position to act on it. Two obstacles stood in his way. He did not know Mr. Edison, and he did not have enough money to pay his railroad fare to Orange, New Jersey. These obstacles would have discouraged most people. But his was no ordinary desire. He was so determined to find a way to carry out his desire that he finally decided to travel by "blind baggage," rather than be defeated. (To the uninitiated, this means that he went to East Orange on a freight train). He presented himself at Mr. Edison's laboratory and announced he had come to go into business with the inventor. In speaking of the first meeting between Barnes and Edison, years later, Mr. Edison said, "He stood there before me, looking like an ordinary beggar, *but there was something in the expression of his face which conveyed the impression that he was determined to get what he had come after*. I had learned, from years of experience, that when someone really DESIRES a thing so deeply that he is willing to stake his entire future on a single turn of the wheel in order to get it, he is sure to win. I gave him the opportunity he asked for, *because I saw he had made up his mind to try until he succeeded*. Subsequent events proved that no mistake was made."

The words young Barnes spoke were far less important than that what he was thinking. Edison, himself, said so. It could not have been the young man's appearance that got him his start in the Edison office, for that was definitely against him. It was what he THOUGHT that counted. If the significance of this statement could be conveyed to every person who reads it, there would be no need for the rest of the book. Barnes did not get his partnership with Edison on his first interview. He did get a chance to work in the Edison offices, at a very nominal wage, doing work that was unimportant to Edison, but very important to Barnes, because it gave him an opportunity to display his "merchandise" where his intended "partner" could see it.

Months went by. Nothing happened to bring realize the goal that Barnes had set up in his mind as his DEFINITE MAJOR PURPOSE. But something important was happening in Barnes' mind. He was constantly intensifying his DESIRE to become Edison's business partner. Psychologists have correctly observed that when someone truly wants to see something, they see it; even it doesn't appear to be there. Barnes was ready for a partnership with Edison. More important, he was DETERMINED TO REMAIN READY UNTIL HE GOT WHAT HE WANTED. He did not say to himself, "Ah well, what's the use? I guess I'll change my mind and try for a sales job." He said, "I came here to go into business with Edison, and I'll reach my goal even if it takes the rest of my life." *He meant it!* What a different story most people would have to tell if only they would adopt a DEFINITE PURPOSE, and stand by that purpose until it became an all-consuming obsession!

Maybe young Barnes did not know it at the time, but his bulldog determination, his persistence in standing behind a single DESIRE, was destined to mow down all opposition and bring him the opportunity he was seeking. When the opportunity came, it appeared in a different form and from a different direction than he had expected. That is one of the tricks of opportunity. It has a sly habit of slipping in by the back door, and often it comes disguised in the form of misfortune or temporary defeat. This is one reason many people fail to recognize opportunities.

Mr. Edison had just perfected a new device, known at that time, as the Edison Dictating Machine (now the Ediphone). His sales people were not enthusiastic over the machine and were convinced it would be hard to sell. Barnes saw his opportunity. It had crawled in quietly, hidden in a strange new machine that interested no one but Barnes and the inventor. Barnes knew he could sell the Edison Dictating Machine. He suggested this to Edison and promptly got his chance. He did sell the machine. In fact, he sold it so successfully that Edison gave him a contract to distribute and market it all over the nation. Out of that business association grew the slogan, "Made by Edison and installed by Barnes." The partnership worked for decades. Out of it Barnes made himself wealthy, but also did something infinitely greater, he proved that you really can, "Think and Grow Rich."

How much actual cash that original DESIRE of Barnes' has been worth to him, I have no way of knowing. It has likely brought him several million dollars, but the amount, whatever may be, is insignificant when compared with the greater asset he acquired in the form of definite knowledge that *an intangible impulse of thought can be transformed into its physical counterpart* by applying known principles. Barnes literally *thought* himself into a partnership with the great Edison! He thought himself into a fortune. He had nothing to start with, except the capacity to KNOW WHAT HE WANTED AND THE DETERMINATION TO STAND BY THAT DESIRE UNTIL HE REALIZED IT. He had no money to begin with. He had very little education. He had no influence. But he did have initiative, faith, and the will to win.

With these intangible forces, he *made himself* number one with the greatest inventor who ever lived.

CHAPTER 1

DESIRE

THE STARTING POINT OF ALL ACHIEVEMENT

WHEN EDWIN C. BARNES climbed down from the freight train in Orange, N. J., he may have resembled a beggar, but his *thoughts* were those of a king. As he made his way from the railroad tracks to Thomas A. Edison's office, his mind was at work. He saw himself *standing in Edison's presence*. He heard himself asking Mr. Edison for an opportunity to carry out the one CONSUMING OBSESSION OF HIS LIFE, a BURNING DESIRE to become the business associate of the great inventor.

Barnes' desire was not a *hope!* It was not a *wish!* It was a keen, pulsating DESIRE, which transcended everything else. It was DEFINITE. The desire was not new when he approached Edison. It had been Barnes' *dominating desire* for a long time. In the beginning, when the desire first appeared in his mind, it may have been, probably was, only a wish, but it was no mere wish when he appeared before Edison with it.

A few years later, Edwin C. Barnes again stood before Edison, in the same office where he first met the inventor. This time his DESIRE had been translated into reality. *He was in business with Edison.* The dominating DREAM OF HIS LIFE had become a reality. Today, people envy Barnes, because of his "lucky break." They see him in the days of his triumph, without taking the trouble to investigate the *cause* of his success. Barnes succeeded because he chose a definite goal, placed all his energy, all his will power, all his effort, everything behind that goal. He did not become the partner of Edison the day he arrived. He was content to start in the most menial work, as long as it provided an opportunity to take even one step toward his cherished goal.

Five years passed before the chance he had been seeking made its appearance. During all those years not one ray of hope, not one promise of attainment of his DESIRE had been held out to him. To everyone, except himself, he appeared only another cog in the Edison business wheel, but in his own mind, HE WAS THE PARTNER OF EDISON EVERY MINUTE OF THE TIME, from the very day that he first went to work there.

It is a remarkable illustration of the power of a DEFINITE DESIRE. Barnes won his goal, because he wanted to be a business associate of Mr. Edison more than he wanted anything else. He created a plan by which to attain that purpose. But he BURNED ALL BRIDGES BEHIND HIM. He stood by his DESIRE until it became the dominating obsession of his life—and—finally, a fact. When he went to Orange, he did not say to himself, "I will try to induce Edison to give me a job of some sort." He said, "I will see Edison, and make sure he knows that I have come to go into business with him."

He did not say, "I will work there for a few months, and if I get no encouragement, I will quit and get a job somewhere else." He did say, "I will start anywhere. I will do anything Edison tells me to do, but *before I am through*, I will be his associate." He did not say, "I will keep my eyes open for another opportunity, in case I fail to get what I want in the Edison organization." He said, "There is but ONE thing in this world that I am determined to have, and that is a business association with Thomas A. Edison. I will burn all bridges behind me, and stake my ENTIRE FUTURE on my ability to get what I want."

He left himself no possible way of retreat. He had to win or perish! That is all there is to the Barnes story of success!

Long ago, a great warrior faced a situation that made it necessary for him to make a decision that insured his success on the battlefield. He was about to send his armies against a powerful enemy, whose men outnumbered his own. He loaded his soldiers into boats, sailed to the enemy's country, unloaded soldiers and equipment, then gave the order to burn the ships that had carried them. Addressing his men before the first battle, he said, "You see the boats going up in smoke. That means that we cannot leave these shores alive unless we win! We now have no choice—*we win or we perish!* They won.

Every person who wins in any undertaking must be willing to burn the ships and cut all sources of retreat. Only by so doing can you be sure of maintain that state of mind known as a BURNING DESIRE TO WIN, essential to success. The morning after the great Chicago fire, a group of merchants stood on State Street, looking at the smoking remains of what had been their stores. They went into a conference to decide if they would try to rebuild, or leave Chicago and start over in a more promising section of the country. They reached a decision—all except one—to leave Chicago.

The merchant who decided to stay and rebuild pointed a finger at the remains of his store, and said, "On that very spot I will build the world's greatest store, no matter how many times it may burn down."

That was more than fifty years ago. The store was built. It stands there today, a towering monument to the power of that state of mind known as a BURNING DESIRE. The easy thing for Marshal Field to have done, would have been exactly what his fellow merchants did. When the going was hard, and the future looked dismal, they pulled up and went where the going seemed easier. Remember this difference between Marshal Field and the other merchants, because it is the same difference which distinguishes Edwin C. Barnes from thousands of other young men who have worked in the Edison organization. It is the same difference that distinguishes practically all who succeed from those who fail. Every human being who reaches the age of understanding of the purpose of money, wishes for it. *Wishing* will not bring riches. But *desiring* riches with a state of mind that becomes an obsession, then planning definite ways and means to acquire riches, and backing those plans with persistence which *does not recognize failure*, will bring riches.

It is important that you follow the instructions described in six steps on the following pages. It is especially important that you observe, and follow the instructions in the sixth step. You may complain that it is impossible for you to "see yourself in possession of money" before you actually have it. Here is where a BURNING DESIRE will come to your aid. If you truly DESIRE money so keenly that your desire is an obsession, you will have no difficulty in convincing yourself that you will acquire it. The object is to want money, and to become so determined to have it that you CONVINCE yourself you will have it. Only those who become "money conscious" ever accumulate great riches. "Money consciousness" means that your mind has become so thoroughly saturated with the DESIRE for money, that you can see yourself already in possession of it.

To the uninitiated, who have not been schooled in the working principles of the human mind, these instructions may appear impractical. It may be helpful, to all who fail to recognize the soundness of the six steps, to know that the information they convey, was received from Andrew Carnegie, who began as an ordinary laborer in the steel mills, but managed, despite his humble beginning, to make these principles yield him a fortune over one hundred million dollars. It may be of further help to know that the six steps were carefully scrutinized by the late Thomas A. Edison, who placed his stamp of approval on them as being, not only the steps essential for the accumulation of money, but necessary for the attainment of *any definite goal*.

DESIRE TO WEALTH IN SIX STEPS

1. Define the *exact* amount of money you desire. It is not sufficient merely to say, "I want plenty of money." Be specific as to the amount. (There is a psychological reason for definiteness that will be explained later).

2. Determine exactly what you intend to give in return for the money you desire. (There is no such thing as something for nothing.)

3. Establish a definite date when you intend to *possess* the money you desire.

4. Create a definite plan for carrying out your desire and begin *at once*, whether you are ready or not, to put this plan into *action*. How will you begin? What are the first steps you need to take? Do you require any further knowledge or skill? How will you obtain them? What existing relationships will help you? What relationships do you need to improve/create?

5. DEFINE YOUR CHIEF AIM. Write out a clear, concise statement of the amount of money you intend to acquire, name the time limit for its acquisition, state what you intend to give in return for the money, and HOW you intend to accumulate it.

6. Read your written statement aloud, twice daily, once just before retiring at night, and once after arising in the morning. AS YOU READ—SEE AND FEEL AND BELIEVE YOURSELF ALREADY IN POSSESSION OF THE MONEY.

The steps call for no hard labor. They call for no sacrifice. They do not require one to become ridiculous or credulous. To apply them calls for no great amount of education. But the successful application of these six steps does call for sufficient *imagination* to enable one to see, and to understand, that accumulation of money cannot be left to chance, good fortune, and luck. One must realize that all who have accumulated great fortunes, first did a certain amount of dreaming, hoping, wishing, DESIRING, and PLANNING *before* they acquired money. You may as well know, right here, that you can never have riches in great quantities, UNLESS you can work yourself into a white heat of DESIRE for money, and actually BELIEVE you will possess it. You may as well know, also that every great leader, from the dawn of civilization down to the present, was a dreamer.

If you do not see great riches in your imagination, you will never see them in your bank balance. Never, in the history of America has there been so much opportunity for practical dreamers as there is now. The economic collapse has reduced everyone, substantially, to the same level. A new race is about to be run. The stakes represent huge fortunes, which will be accumulated within the next ten years. The rules of the race have changed, because we now live in a CHANGED WORLD. We who are in this race for wealth, should be encouraged to know that this changed world in which we live is demanding new ideas, new ways of doing things, new leaders, new inventions, new methods of teaching, new methods of marketing, new books, new technologies. Behind all this demand for new and better things, there is one quality that you need to win, and that is DEFINITENESS OF PURPOSE, the knowledge of what you want, and a burning DESIRE to possess it.

The business depression marked the death of one age, and the birth of another. This changed world requires practical visionaries who can, *and will* put their dreams into action. The practical visionaries have always been, and always will be the pattern-makers of civilization. Those who desire to accumulate wealth, should remember the real leaders of the world have always been those who harnessed, and put into practical use, the intangible, unseen forces of unborn opportunity, and have converted those forces, (or impulses of thought), into sky-scrapers, cities, airplanes, automobiles, computers, cell phones, and every form of convenience that makes life more pleasant. Tolerance and an open mind are necessities for today's visionaries. Those who are afraid of new ideas are doomed before they start. Never has there been a time more favorable to entrepreneurs than the present. True, there is no wild and woolly west to be conquered, as in the days of the Covered Wagon; but there is a vast business, financial, and industrial world to be remodeled and redirected along new and better lines.

In planning to acquire your share of wealth, you must catch the spirit of the great visionary leaders of the past, whose dreams have given to civilization all that it has of value, the spirit which serves as the life-blood of our own country—your opportunity and mine, to develop and market our talents. Copernicus, the great astronomer, dreamed of a multiplicity of worlds, and revealed them! No one denounced him as "impractical" *after* he had triumphed. Instead, the world worshipped at his shrine, thus proving once more that SUCCESS REQUIRES NO APOLOGIES and FAILURE PERMITS NO ALIBIS. If the thing you wish to do is right, and you believe in it, go ahead and do it! Put your dream across, and never mind what "they" say if you meet with temporary defeat, for "they," perhaps, do not know that EVERY FAILURE BRINGS WITH IT THE SEED OF AN EQUIVALENT SUCCESS.

Henry Ford, poor and uneducated, dreamed of a horseless carriage, went to work with what tools he possessed, without waiting for opportunity to favor him, and now evidence of his dream belts the entire earth. He has put more wheels into operation than anyone who ever lived, because he was not afraid to back his dreams. Thomas Edison dreamed of a lamp that could be operated by electricity, began where he stood to put his dream into action, and despite more than *ten thousand failures*, he stood by that dream until he made it a physical reality. Practical dreamers DO NOT QUIT! Lincoln dreamed of freedom for slaves, put his dream into action, and barely missed living to see a united North and South translate his dream into reality. The Wright brothers dreamed of a machine that would fly through the air. Now one may see evidence all over the world that they dreamed soundly. Marconi dreamed of a system for harnessing the intangible forces of the ether. Evidence that he did not dream in vain, may be found in every wireless and radio in the world. Moreover, Marconi's dream brought the humblest cabin, and the largest mansion side by side. It made the people of every nation on earth back-door neighbors. It gave the President of the United States a medium by which he could talk to all the people of America at one time, and on short notice. It may interest you to know that Marconi's "friends" had him taken into custody and examined in a psychopathic hospital, when he announced he had discovered a principle through which he could send messages through the air, without the aid of wires, or other direct physical means of communication. The dreamers of today fare better.

The world has become accustomed to new discoveries. It has shown a willingness to reward the visionary who gives the world a new idea. The greatest achievement was, at first, and for a time, but a dream. The oak sleeps in the acorn. The bird waits in the egg, and in the highest vision of the soul, a waking angel stirs. DREAMS ARE THE SEEDLINGS OF REALITY. Awake, arise, and assert yourself, you dreamers of the world. Your star is rising. The world-wide economic collapse brought the opportunity you have been waiting for. It has taught people humility, tolerance, and open-mindedness.

The world is filled with an abundance of OPPORTUNITY that the dreamers of the past never knew. A BURNING DESIRE TO BE AND TO DO is the starting point from which the dreamer must take off. Dreams are not born of indifference, laziness, or lack of ambition. The world no longer scoffs at dreamers, nor calls them impractical. If you think it does, take a look at the 2008 American presidential election. For the first time in the history of our country, the nation elected an African-American president. Not a man from a privileged background. A man from humble beginnings with the name Barack Hussein Obama. The world has shown its readiness to get behind big thinkers and big dreamers.

You may have been disappointed; you have suffered defeat during the economic collapse. You may have felt the great heart within you crushed until it bled. Take courage, for these experiences have strengthened your spiritual metal; they are assets of incomparable value. Remember, too, that all who succeed in life get off to a bad start, and pass through many heartbreaking struggles before they "arrive." The turning point in the lives of those who succeed, usually comes at the moment of some crisis, through which they are introduced to their "other selves."

John Bunyan wrote the Pilgrim's Progress, which is among the finest of all English literature, after he had been confined in prison and sorely punished, because of his views on the subject of religion. O. Henry discovered the genius, which slept within his brain, after he had met with great misfortune, and was confined in a prison cell, in Columbus, Ohio. Being FORCED, through misfortune, to become acquainted with his "other self," and to use his IMAGINATION, he discovered himself to be a great author instead of a miserable criminal and outcast. Strange and varied are the ways of life, and stranger still are the ways of Infinite Intelligence, through which we are sometimes forced to undergo all sorts of punishment before discovering our own brains, and our own capacity to create useful ideas through imagination.

Edison, the world's greatest inventor and scientist, was a low-wage telegraph operator; he failed countless times before he was driven, finally, to the discovery of the genius that slept within his brain. Charles Dickens began by pasting labels on blacking pots. The tragedy of his first love penetrated the depths of his soul, and converted him into one of the world's truly great authors. That tragedy produced, first, *David Copperfield*, then a succession of other works that made this a richer and better world for all who read his books. Disappointment over love affairs generally has the effect of driving people to drink and into ruin; and this, because most people never learn the art of transforming their strongest emotions into dreams of a constructive nature.

Helen Keller became deaf, dumb, and blind shortly after birth. Despite her greatest misfortune, she has written her name indelibly in the pages of the history of the great. Her entire life has served as evidence that *no one ever is defeated until defeat has been accepted as a reality*. Robert Burns was an illiterate country boy; he was cursed by poverty and grew up to be a drunk in the bargain. The world was made better for his having lived, because he clothed beautiful thoughts in poetry, and thereby plucked a thorn and planted a rose in its place. Booker T. Washington was born in slavery, handicapped by race and color. Because he was tolerant, had an open mind at all times, on all subjects, and was a DREAMER, he left his impression for good on an entire race. Beethoven was deaf, Milton was blind, but their names will last as long as time endures, because they dreamed and translated their dreams into organized thought. Nelson Mandela spent twenty-seven years in jail, before he successfully negotiated and dismantled the apartheid regime in South Africa. Even under impossible circumstances, he did not give up his dream.

Before passing to the next chapter, start the fire in your mind of hope, faith, courage, and tolerance. If you have these states of mind, and a working knowledge of the principles described, all else that you need will come to you when you are READY for it. There is a difference between WISHING for a thing and being READY to receive it. No one is *ready* for a thing, until he *believes* he can acquire it. The state of mind must be BELIEF, not mere hope or wish. Open-mindedness is essential for belief. Closed minds do not inspire faith, courage, or belief. Remember, no more effort is required to aim high in life, to demand abundance and prosperity, than is required to accept misery and poverty. A great poet has correctly stated this universal truth through these lines:

> I bargained with Life for a penny,
> And Life would pay no more,
> However I begged at evening
> When I counted my scanty store.
>
> For Life is a just employer,
> He gives you what you ask,
> But once you have set the wages,
> Why, you must bear the task.
>
> I worked for a menial's hire,
> Only to learn, dismayed,
> That any wage I had asked of Life,
> Life would have willingly paid.

Several years ago, one of my business associates became ill. He became worse as time went on, and finally was taken to the hospital for an operation. Just before he was wheeled into the operating room, I took a look at him, and wondered how anyone as thin and emaciated as he, could possibly go through a major operation successfully. The doctor warned me that there was little if any chance of my ever seeing him alive again. But that was the DOCTOR'S OPINION. It was not the opinion of the patient. Just before he was wheeled away, he whispered feebly, "Do not be disturbed, Chief, I will be out of here in a few days." The attending nurse looked at me with pity. But the patient did come through safely. After it was all over, his physician said, "Nothing but his own desire to live saved him. He never would have pulled through if he had not refused to accept the possibility of death."

I believe in the power of DESIRE backed by FAITH, because I have seen this power lift people from lowly beginnings to places of power and wealth; I have seen it rob the grave of its victims; I have seen it serve as the medium by which people stage a comeback after having been defeated in a hundred different ways; I have seen it provide my own son with a normal, happy, successful life, despite nature's having sent him into the world without ears. How can one harness and use the power of DESIRE? This has been answered through this, and the subsequent chapters of this book. This message is going out to the world at the end of the most devastating economic collapses America has ever known. It is reasonable to presume that the message may come to the attention of many who have been wounded by the economy, those who have lost their fortunes, others who have lost their jobs or their retirement savings, and great numbers who must reorganize their plans and stage a comeback. To all these I wish to convey the thought that all achievement, no matter what may be its nature, or its purpose, must begin with an intense, BURNING DESIRE for something definite.

Through some strange and powerful principle of "mental chemistry" which it has never divulged, nature wraps up in the impulse of STRONG DESIRE "that something" which recognizes no such word as impossible and accepts no such reality as failure.

CHAPTER 2

FAITH

VISUALIZATION AND BELIEF IN ATTAINMENT OF DESIRE

FAITH IS THE head chemist of the mind. When FAITH is blended with the vibration of thought, the subconscious mind instantly picks up the vibration, translates it into its spiritual equivalent, and transmits it to Infinite Intelligence, as in the case of prayer. The emotions of FAITH, LOVE, and SEX are the most powerful of all the major positive emotions. When the three are blended, they have the effect of "coloring" the vibration of thought in such a way that it instantly reaches the subconscious mind, where it is changed into its spiritual equivalent, the only form that induces a response from Infinite Intelligence. Love and faith are psychic; related to the spiritual side. Sex is purely biological, and related only to the physical. The mixing, or blending, of these three emotions has the effect of opening a direct line of communication between the finite, thinking mind, and Infinite Intelligence.

DEVELOPING FAITH

There comes, now, a statement which will give a better understanding of the importance the principle of auto-suggestion assumes in the transformation of desire into its physical, or monetary equivalent; namely: FAITH is a state of mind which may be induced, or created, by affirmation or repeated instructions to the subconscious mind, through the principle of auto-suggestion. As an illustration, consider the purpose for which you are, presumably, reading this book. The object is, naturally, to acquire the ability to transform the intangible thought impulse of DESIRE into its physical counterpart, money. By following the instructions laid down in the chapters on auto-suggestion, and the subconscious mind, as summarized in the chapter on auto-suggestion, you may CONVINCE the subconscious mind that you believe you will receive that for which you ask, and it will act on that belief, which your subconscious mind passes back to you in the form of "FAITH," followed by definite plans for procuring that which you desire.

The method by which one develops FAITH, where it does not already exist, is extremely difficult to describe, almost as difficult, in fact, as it would be to describe the color of red to a blind person who has never seen color, and has no context for understanding it. Faith is a state of mind that you may develop at will after you have mastered the thirteen principles, because it is a state of mind that develops voluntarily, through application and use of these principles. *Repetition of affirmation of orders to your subconscious mind is the only known method of voluntary development of faith.* Perhaps the meaning may be made clearer through the following explanation as to the way people sometimes become criminals. In the words of a criminologist, "When people first come into contact with crime, they dislike it. If they remain in contact with crime for a time, they become accustomed to it, and endure it. If they remain in contact with it long enough, they finally embrace it and become influenced by it."

This is the equivalent of saying that any impulse of thought which is repeatedly passed on to the subconscious mind is, finally, accepted and acted on by the subconscious mind, which proceeds to translate that impulse into its physical equivalent, by the most practical procedure available. In connection with this, consider again the statement, ALL THOUGHTS WHICH HAVE BEEN EMOTIONALIZED, (given feeling) AND MIXED WITH FAITH, begin immediately to translate themselves into their physical equivalent or counterpart. The emotions, or the "feeling" portion of thoughts, give thoughts vitality, life, and action. The emotions of Faith, Love, and Sex, when mixed with any thought impulse, give it greater action than any of these emotions can do on its own. Not only thought impulses which have been mixed with FAITH, but those which have been mixed with any of the positive emotions, or any of the negative emotions, may reach, and influence the subconscious mind. From this statement, you will understand that the subconscious mind will translate into its physical equivalent, a thought impulse of a negative or destructive nature, just as readily as it will act on thought impulses of a positive or constructive nature. This accounts for the strange phenomenon that so many millions of people experience, referred to as "misfortune," or "bad luck."

There are millions of people who BELIEVE themselves "doomed" to poverty and failure, because of some strange force over which they BELIEVE they have no control. They are the creators of their own "misfortunes," because of this negative BELIEF, which is picked up by the subconscious mind and translated into its physical equivalent. This is an appropriate place to suggest again that you may benefit, by passing on to your subconscious mind, any DESIRE you wish translated into its physical, or monetary equivalent, in a state of expectancy or BELIEF that the transformation will actually take place. Your BELIEF, or FAITH, is the element that determines the action of your subconscious mind. There is nothing to hinder you from "deceiving" your subconscious mind when giving it instructions through autosuggestion, as I deceived my son's subconscious mind. To make this "deception" more realistic, conduct yourself just as you would, if you were ALREADY IN POSSESSION OF THE MATERIAL THING YOU ARE DEMANDING. The subconscious mind will transform into its physical equivalent, by the most direct and practical media available, any order which is given to it in a state of BELIEF, or FAITH, that the order will be carried out.

Surely, enough has been stated to give a starting point for mixing FAITH with any order given to the subconscious mind. Perfection will come through practice. It *cannot* come by merely *reading* instructions. If a person can become a criminal by association with crime, (and this is a known fact), it is equally true that one may develop faith by voluntarily suggesting to the subconscious mind that one has faith. The mind comes, finally, to take on the nature of the influences that dominate it. Understand this truth, and you will know why it is essential for you to encourage the *positive emotions* as dominating forces of your mind, and to discourage and *eliminate* negative emotions. A mind dominated by positive emotions, becomes a favorable home for faith. A mind so dominated may, at will, give the subconscious mind instructions, which it will accept and act on immediately.

FAITH AND AUTO-SUGGESTION

All down the ages, the religionists have told humanity to "have faith" in this, that, and the other dogma or creed, but they have failed to tell people HOW to have faith. They have not stated that faith is a state of mind, and that it may be induced by self-suggestion. In language that any normal human being can understand, we will describe all that is known about the principle through which FAITH may be developed, where it does not already exist.

Have Faith in yourself; Faith in the Infinite. Before we begin, you should be reminded again that: FAITH is the "eternal elixir" which gives life, power, and action to the impulse of thought!

FAITH is the starting point of all accumulation of riches!

FAITH is the basis of all "miracles," and all mysteries that cannot be analyzed by the rules of science!

FAITH is the only known antidote for FAILURE!

FAITH is the element, the "chemical" which, when mixed with prayer, gives one direct communication with Infinite Intelligence.

FAITH is the element that transforms the ordinary vibration of thought, created by the finite mind of humans, into the spiritual equivalent.

FAITH is the only agency through which the cosmic force of Infinite Intelligence can be harnessed and used.

EVERY ONE OF THE PREVIOUS STATEMENTS CAN BE PROVEN! The proof is simple and easily demonstrated. It is wrapped up in the principle of auto-suggestion. Let us center our attention, therefore, on self-suggestion, and find out what it is, and what it is capable of achieving. It is a well known fact that we eventually BELIEVE whatever we repeat to ourselves, *whether it is true or not*. If a person repeats a lie over and over, they will eventually accept the lie as truth. Moreover, they will BELIEVE it to be the truth. We are who we are because of the DOMINATING

THOUGHTS we permit to occupy our minds. Thoughts that we deliberately place in our own minds, and encourage with sympathy, and with which we mix any one or more of the emotions, constitute the motivating forces, which direct and control our every movement, act, and endeavor!

THOUGHTS MIXED WITH ANY FEELINGS OR EMOTIONS, CONSTITUTE A "MAGNETIC" FORCE THAT ATTRACTS, FROM THE VIBRATIONS OF THE ETHER, OTHER SIMILAR OR RELATED THOUGHTS. A thought "magnetized" with emotion may be compared to a seed which, when planted in fertile soil, germinates, grows, and multiplies itself over and over again, until that which was originally one small seed, becomes countless millions of seeds of the SAME PLANT! The ether is a great cosmic mass of eternal forces of vibration. It is made up of both destructive vibrations and constructive vibrations. It carries, at all times, vibrations of fear, poverty, disease, failure, misery; and vibrations of prosperity, health, success, and happiness, just as surely as it carries the sound of hundreds of orchestrations of music, and hundreds of human voices, all of which maintain their own individuality and means of identification through the medium of radio. From the great storehouse of the ether, the human mind is constantly attracting vibrations that harmonize with that which DOMINATES the human mind. Any thought, idea, plan, or purpose which one *holds* in one's mind attracts, from the vibrations of the ether, a host of its relatives, adds these "relatives" to its own force, and grows until it becomes the dominating, MOTIVATING MASTER of the individual in whose mind it has been housed.

Now, let us go back to the starting point, and become informed as to how the original seed of an idea, plan, or purpose may be planted in the mind. The information is easily conveyed: any idea, plan, or purpose may be placed in the mind *through repetition of thought*. This is why you are asked to write out a statement of your major purpose, or Definite Chief Aim, commit it to memory, and repeat it, in audible words, day after day, until these vibrations of sound have reached your subconscious mind. We are what we are, because of the vibrations of thought which we pick up and register, in our daily environment. Resolve to throw off the influences of any unfortunate environment and to build your own life to ORDER. Taking inventory of mental assets and liabilities, you will discover that your greatest weakness is lack of self-confidence. This handicap can be surmounted, and timidity translated into courage, through the aid of the principle of autosuggestion. The application of this principle may be made through a simple arrangement of positive thought impulses stated in writing, memorized, and repeated, until they become a part of the working equipment of the subconscious faculty of your mind.

Behind the self-confidence formula, on the following page, is a law of Nature which has yet been to be explained. It has baffled scientists of all ages. Psychologists have named this law "auto-suggestion," and let it go at that. The name of the law is of little importance. What's important is that it WORKS for the glory and success of mankind, IF it is used constructively. On the other hand, if used destructively, it will destroy just as readily. In this statement may be found a very significant truth, namely; that those who go down in defeat, and end their lives in poverty, misery, and distress, do so because of negative application of the principle of auto-suggestion. The cause may be found in the fact that ALL IMPULSES OF THOUGHT HAVE A TENDENCY TO CLOTHE THEMSELVES IN THEIR PHYSICAL EQUIVALENT.

The subconscious mind, (the chemical laboratory where all thought impulses are combined and made ready for translation into physical reality), makes no distinction between constructive and destructive thought impulses. It works with the material we feed it, through our thought impulses. The subconscious mind will translate into reality a thought driven by FEAR just as readily as it will translate into reality a thought driven by COURAGE, or FAITH.

FORMULA for SELF-CONFIDENCE

First. I know that I have the ability to achieve the object of my Definite Purpose in life, therefore, I DEMAND of myself persistent, continuous action toward its attainment, and I here and now promise to render such action.

Second. I realize the dominating thoughts of my mind will eventually reproduce themselves in outward, physical action, and gradually transform themselves into physical reality, therefore, I will concentrate my thoughts for thirty minutes daily, upon the task of thinking of the person I intend to become, thereby creating in my mind a clear mental picture of that person.

Third. I know through the principle of auto-suggestion, any desire that I persistently hold in my mind will eventually seek expression through some practical means of attaining the object back of it, therefore, I will devote ten minutes daily to demanding of myself the development of SELF-CONFIDENCE.

Fourth. I have clearly written down a description of my DEFINITE CHIEF AIM in life, and I will never stop trying, until I shall have developed sufficient self-confidence for its attainment.

Fifth. I fully realize that no wealth or position can last, unless built honestly, therefore, I will engage in no transaction which does not benefit all whom it affects. I will succeed by attracting the forces I wish to use, and the cooperation of other people. I will induce others to serve me, because of my willingness to serve others. I will eliminate hatred, envy, jealousy, selfishness, and cynicism, by developing love for all humanity, because I know that a negative attitude toward others can never bring me success. I will cause others to believe in me, because I will believe in them, and in myself.

The pages of medical history are rich with cases of "suggestive suicide." A person can commit suicide through negative suggestion, just as effectively as by any other means. In a Midwestern city, a man by the name of Joseph Grant, a bank official, "borrowed" a large sum of the bank's money, without the consent of the directors. He lost the money through gambling. One afternoon, the Bank Examiner came to check the accounts. Grant left the bank, took a room in a local hotel, and when they found him, three days later, he was lying in bed, wailing and moaning, repeating over and over, "My God, this will kill me! I cannot stand the disgrace." In a short time, he was dead. The doctors pronounced the first case of "mental suicide."

Just as electricity will turn the wheels of industry, and is useful when used constructively; or snuff out life if wrongly used, so will the law of auto-suggestion lead you to peace and prosperity, or down into the valley of misery, failure, and death, according to your degree of understanding and application of it. If you fill your mind with FEAR, doubt, and lacking belief in your ability to connect with and use the forces of Infinite Intelligence, the law of auto-suggestion will take this spirit of unbelief and use it as a pattern by which your subconscious mind will translate it into its physical equivalent. THIS STATEMENT IS AS TRUE AS THE STATEMENT THAT TWO AND TWO ARE FOUR!

Like the wind that carries one ship East, and another West, the law of auto-suggestion will lift you up or pull you down, according to the way you set your sails of THOUGHT. The law of auto-suggestion, through which any person may rise to altitudes of achievement which stagger the imagination, is well described in the following verse:

If you *think* you are beaten, you are,
If you *think* you dare not, you don't.
If you like to win, but you *think* you can't,
It is almost certain you won't.
If you *think* you'll lose, you're lost
For out of the world we find,
Success begins with a fellow's will—
It's all in the *state of mind*.
If you *think* you are outclassed, you are,
You've got to *think* high to rise,
You've got to *be sure of yourself* before
You can ever win a prize.
Life's battles don't always go
To the stronger or faster one,
But eventually, the one who wins
Is the one WHO THINKS HE CAN!

Observe the words which have been emphasized, and you will catch the deep meaning which the poet had in mind.

Somewhere in your make-up (perhaps in the cells of your brain) there lies *sleeping*, the seed of achievement that, if aroused and put into action, would carry you to heights you may never have hoped to attain. Just as a master musician may cause the most beautiful strains of music to pour from the strings of a violin, you can arouse the genius that lies asleep in your brain and cause it to drive you upward to whatever goal you may wish to achieve. Abraham Lincoln was a failure at everything he tried, until he was well past the age of forty. He was a Mr. Nobody from Nowhere, until a great experience came into his life, aroused the sleeping genius within his heart and brain, and gave the world one of its really great men. That "experience" was mixed with the emotions of sorrow and LOVE. It came to him through Anne Rutledge, the only woman he ever truly loved.

It is a known fact that the emotion of LOVE is closely related to the state of mind known as FAITH, and this for the reason that Love comes very near to translating one's thought impulses into their spiritual equivalent. If you need evidence for the power of FAITH, study the achievements of those who have employed it. At the head of the list comes the Nazarene. The basis of Christianity is FAITH, no matter how many people may have perverted, or misinterpreted the meaning of this great force, and no matter how many dogmas and creeds has been created in its name, which do not reflect its tenets. The sum and substance of the teachings and the achievements of Christ, which may have been interpreted as "miracles," were nothing more nor less than FAITH. If there are any such phenomena as "miracles" they are produced only through the state of mind known as FAITH! Some teachers of religion, and many who call themselves Christians, neither understand nor practice FAITH.

Let us consider the power of FAITH, as it is now being demonstrated, by a man who is well known to all of civilization, Mahatma Gandhi, of India. In this man, the world has one of the most astounding examples known to civilization, of the possibilities of FAITH. Despite the fact that he has none of the orthodox tools of power, such as money, battle ships, soldiers, and materials of warfare, Gandhi wields more potential power than most people on the earth, combined. Gandhi has no money, he has no home, he does not own a suit of clothes, but HE DOES HAVE POWER. How does he come by that power?

HE CREATED IT OUT OF HIS UNDERSTANDING OF THE PRINCIPLE OF FAITH, AND THROUGH HIS ABILITY TO TRANSPLANT THAT FAITH INTO THE MINDS OF TWO HUNDRED MILLION PEOPLE.

Gandhi has accomplished, through the influence of FAITH, that which the strongest military power on earth could not, and never will accomplish through soldiers and military equipment. He has accomplished the astounding feat of INFLUENCING two hundred million minds to COALESCE AND MOVE IN UNISON, AS A SINGLE MIND. What other force on earth, except FAITH could do this?

There will come a day when employees as well as employers will discover the possibilities of FAITH. That day is dawning. The whole world has had ample opportunity, during the recent business depression, to witness what the LACK OF FAITH will do to the economy. Surely, civilization has produced a sufficient number of intelligent human beings to make use of this great lesson that the depression has taught the world. During this period, the world had evidence that widespread FEAR will paralyze the wheels of industry and business. Out of this experience will arise leaders in business and industry who will profit by the example Gandhi set for the world, and they will apply to business the same tactics he has used in building the greatest following known in the history of the world.

Business is due for a reform, make no mistake about this! The methods of the past, based upon economic combinations of FORCE and FEAR, will be supplanted by the better principles of FAITH and cooperation. The economy WILL BE LED BY LEADERS WHO UNDERSTAND AND APPLY THE PRINCIPLES EMPLOYED BY MAHATMA GANDHI. Only in this way will leaders get FULL cooperation which constitutes power in its highest and most enduring form. This stupendous information age in which we live, has taken the soul out of people. The watchword of the future will be HUMAN HAPPINESS AND CONTENTMENT, and when this state of mind is attained, the production will take care of itself, more effectively than anything that has ever been accomplished where people did not, and could not mix FAITH and individual interest with their work. Because of the need for faith and cooperation in business, we will analyze the method by which business people accumulate great fortunes, by *giving* before they try to *get*.

The event chosen for this illustration dates back to 1900, when the United States Steel Corporation was being formed. As you read the story, keep in mind these fundamental facts and you will understand how IDEAS have been converted into huge fortunes.

First, the huge United States Steel Corporation was born in the mind of Charles M. Schwab, in the form of an IDEA he created through his IMAGINATION!

Second, he mixed FAITH with his IDEA.

Third, he formulated a PLAN for the transformation of his IDEA into physical and financial reality.

Fourth, he put his plan into action with his famous speech at the University Club.

Fifth, he applied, and followed-through on his PLAN with PERSISTENCE, and backed it with firm DECISION until it had been fully carried out.

Sixth, he prepared the way for success by a BURNING DESIRE for success.

If you are one of those who have often wondered how great fortunes are accumulated, this story of the United States Steel Corporation will be enlightening. If you have any doubt that people can THINK AND GROW RICH, this story should dispel that doubt, because you can plainly see in the story of the United States Steel, the application of a major portion of the thirteen principles described in this book. This astounding description of the power of an IDEA was dramatically told by John Lowell, in the New York World-Telegram, with whose courtesy it is here reprinted.

A PRETTY AFTER-DINNER SPEECH FOR A BILLION DOLLARS

When, on the evening of December 12, 1900, some eighty of the nation's financial nobility gathered in the banquet hall of the University Club on Fifth Avenue to do honor to a young man from out West, few people realized they were about to witness the most significant event in American industrial history.

J. Edward Simmons and Charles Stewart Smith, their hearts full of gratitude for the lavish hospitality bestowed on them by Charles M. Schwab during a recent visit to Pittsburgh, had arranged the dinner to introduce the thirty-eight-year-old steel man to eastern banking society. But they didn't expect him to stampede the convention. They warned him, in fact, that New York's stuffed shirts would not be responsive to oratory, and that, if he didn't want to bore the Stillmans and Harrimans and Vanderbilts, he had better limit himself to fifteen or twenty minutes of polite vaporings and let it go at that.

There was little conversation and what there was of it was restrained. Few of the bankers and brokers had met Schwab, whose career had flowered along the banks of the Monongahela, and none knew him well. But before the evening was over, they—and with them Money Master Morgan—were to be swept off their feet, and a billion-dollar baby, the United States Steel Corporation, was to be conceived.

After it was over and the gathering was still under its spell, although Schwab had talked for ninety minutes, Morgan led the orator to a recessed window where, dangling their legs from the high, uncomfortable seat, they talked for an hour more.

The magic of the Schwab personality had been turned on, full force, but what was more important and lasting was the full-fledged, clear-cut program he laid down for the aggrandizement of Steel. Many others had tried to interest Morgan in slapping together a steel trust. John W. Gates, the gambler, had urged it, but Morgan distrusted him. The Moore boys, Bill and Jim, Chicago stock jobbers who had glued together a match trust and a cracker corporation, had urged it and failed. Elbert H. Gary, the sanctimonious country lawyer, wanted to foster it, but he wasn't big enough to be impressive. Until Schwab's eloquence took J. P. Morgan to the heights from which he could visualize the solid results of the most daring financial undertaking ever conceived, the project was regarded as a delirious dream of easy-money crackpots.

The financial magnetism to attract thousands of small or inefficiently managed companies into large and competition-crushing combinations had become operative in the steel world through the devices of that jovial business pirate, John W. Gates. Gates had formed the American Steel and Wire Company out of a chain of small concerns, and together with Morgan had created the Federal Steel Company. The National Tube and American Bridge companies were two more Morgan concerns, and the Moore Brothers had forsaken the match and cookie business to form the 'American' group—Tin Plate, Steel Hoop, Sheet Steel—and the National Steel Company.

But by the side of Andrew Carnegie's gigantic vertical trust, a trust owned and operated by fifty-three partners, those other combinations were insignificant. They might combine to their heart's content but the whole lot of them couldn't make a dent in the Carnegie organization, and Morgan knew it.

The eccentric old Scot knew it, too. From the magnificent heights of Skibo Castle he had viewed, first with amusement and then with resentment, the attempts of Morgan's smaller companies to cut into his business. When the attempts became too bold, Carnegie's temper was translated into anger and retaliation. He decided to duplicate *every mill owned by his rivals. He hadn't been interested in wire, pipe, hoops, or sheet. Instead, he was content to sell such companies the raw steel and let them work it into whatever shape they wanted. Now, with Schwab as his chief and able lieutenant, he planned to drive his enemies to the wall.*

So it was that in the speech of Charles M. Schwab, Morgan saw the answer to his problem of combination. A trust without Carnegie—giant of them all—would be no trust at all, a plum pudding, as one writer said, without the plums.

Schwab's speech undoubtedly carried the inference, though not the pledge, that the vast Carnegie enterprise could be brought under the Morgan tent. He talked of the world future for steel, of reorganization for efficiency, of specialization, of the scrapping of unsuccessful mills and concentration of effort on the flourishing properties, of economies in the ore traffic, of economies in overhead and administrative departments, of capturing foreign markets.

More than that, he told the buccaneers among them of the errors of their customary piracy. Their purposes, he inferred, had been to create monopolies, raise prices, and pay themselves fat dividends out of privilege. Schwab condemned the system in his heartiest manner. The shortsightedness of such a policy, he said, lay in the fact that it restricted the market in an era when everything cried for expansion. By cheapening the cost of steel, he argued, an ever-expanding market would be created; more uses for steel would be devised, and a good portion of the world trade could be captured. Actually, though he did not know it, Schwab was an apostle of modern mass production.

The dinner ended. Morgan went home to think about Schwab's rosy predictions. Schwab went back to Pittsburgh to run the steel business while Gary and the rest went back to their stock tickers to fiddle around in anticipation of the next move.

It was not long coming. It took Morgan about one week to digest the feast of reason Schwab had placed before him. When he had assured himself that no financial indigestion was to result, he sent for Schwab-and found that young man rather coy. Mr. Carnegie, Schwab indicated, might not like it if he found his trusted company president had been flirting with the Emperor of Wall Street, the Street on which Carnegie was resolved never to tread. Then it was suggested by John W. Gates the go-between, that if Schwab 'happened' to be in the Bellevue Hotel in Philadelphia, J. P. Morgan might also 'happen' to be there. When Schwab arrived, however, Morgan was inconveniently ill at his New York home, and so, on the elder man's pressing invitation, Schwab went to New York and presented himself at the door of the financier's library.

Now certain economic historians have professed the belief that from the beginning to the end of the drama, the stage was set by Andrew Carnegie-that the dinner to Schwab, the famous speech, the Sunday night conference between Schwab and the Money King, were events arranged by the canny Scot. The truth is exactly the opposite. When Schwab was called in to consummate the deal, he didn't even know whether 'the little boss,' as Andrew was called, would so much as listen to an offer to sell, particularly to a group of men whom Andrew regarded as being endowed with something less than holiness. But Schwab did take into the conference with him, in his own handwriting, six sheets of copper-plate figures, representing to his mind the

THINK AND GROW RICH

physical worth and the potential earning capacity of every steel company he regarded as an essential star in the new metal firmament.

Four men pondered over these figures all night. The chief, of course, was Morgan, steadfast in his belief in the Divine Right of Money. With him was his aristocratic partner, Robert Bacon, a scholar and a gentleman. The third was John W. Gates whom Morgan scorned as a gambler and used as a tool. The fourth was Schwab, who knew more about the processes of making and selling steel than any whole group of men then living. Throughout that conference, the Pittsburgher's figures were never questioned. If he said a company was worth so much, then it was worth that much and no more. He was insistent, too, on including in the combination only those concerns he nominated. He had conceived a corporation in which there would be no duplication, not even to satisfy the greed of friends who wanted to unload their companies on the broad Morgan shoulders. He left out, by design, a number of the larger concerns on which the Walruses and Carpenters of Wall Street had cast hungry eyes.

When dawn came, Morgan rose and straightened his back. Only one question remained.

"Do you think you can persuade Andrew Carnegie to sell?" he asked.

"I can try," said Schwab.

"If you can get him to sell, I will undertake the matter," said Morgan.

So far so good. But would Carnegie sell? How much would he demand? (Schwab thought about $320,000,000). What would he take payment in? Common or preferred stocks? Bonds? Cash? Nobody could raise a third of a billion dollars in cash.

There was a golf game in January on the frost-cracking heath of the St. Andrews links In Westchester, with Andrew bundled up in sweaters against the cold, and Charlie talking volubly, as usual, to keep his spirits up. But no word of business was mentioned until the pair sat down in the cozy warmth of the Carnegie cottage. Then, with the same persuasiveness that had hypnotized eighty millionaires at the University Club, Schwab poured out the glittering promises of retirement in comfort, of untold millions to satisfy the old man's social caprices. Carnegie capitulated, wrote a figure on a slip of paper, handed it to Schwab and said, "all right, that's what we'll sell for."

The figure was approximately $400,000,000, and was reached by taking the $320,000,000 mentioned by Schwab as a basic figure, and adding $80,000,000 to represent the increased capital value over the previous two years.

Later, on the deck of a trans-Atlantic liner, the Scotsman said ruefully to Morgan, "I should have asked you for $100,000,000 more."

"If you had asked for it, you'd have gotten it," Morgan told him cheerfully.

There was an uproar, of course. A British correspondent cabled that the foreign steel world was 'appalled' by the gigantic combination. President Hadley, of Yale, declared that unless trusts were regulated the country might expect an emperor in Washington within the next twenty-five years. But that able stock manipulator, Keene, went at his work of shoving the new stock at the public so vigorously that all the excess water-estimated by some at nearly $600,000,000-was absorbed in a twinkling. So Carnegie *had his millions, and the Morgan syndicate had $62,000,000 for all its 'trouble,' and everyone from Gates to Gary, had their millions.*

The thirty-eight-year-old Schwab had his reward. He was made president of the new corporation and remained in control until 1930.

The dramatic story of "Big Business" you just read, was included because it is a perfect illustration of the method by which *DESIRE CAN BE TRANSFORMED INTO ITS PHYSICAL EQUIVALENT!* I imagine some readers will question the statement that a mere, intangible DESIRE can be converted into its physical equivalent. Doubtless some will say, "You cannot convert NOTHING into SOMETHING!" The answer is in the story of United States Steel. That giant organization was created in the mind of one person. The plan that gave it financial stability was created in the mind of the same person. His FAITH, his DESIRE, his IMAGINATION, his PERSISTENCE were the real ingredients that went into United States Steel. The steel mills and mechanical equipment acquired by the corporation, AFTER IT HAD BEEN BROUGHT INTO LEGAL EXISTENCE, were incidental, but careful analysis will disclose the fact that the appraised value of the properties acquired by the corporation increased in value by an estimated SIX HUNDRED MILLION DOLLARS, by the mere transaction that consolidated them under one management.

In other words, Charles M. Schwab's IDEA, plus the FAITH with which he conveyed it to the minds of J. P. Morgan and the others, was marketed for a profit of approximately $600,000,000. Not an insignificant sum for a single IDEA! The practicability of the philosophy described in this book has been established by the fact that the United States Steel Corporation prospered, and became one of the richest and most powerful corporations in America, employing thousands of people, developing new uses for steel, and opening new markets; thus proving that the $600,000,000 in profit that the Schwab IDEA produced was earned. RICHES begin in the form of THOUGHT!

The amount is limited only by the person in whose mind the THOUGHT is put into motion. FAITH removes limitations! Remember this when you are ready to bargain with Life for whatever it is that you ask as your price for having passed this way. Remember, also, that the person who created the United States Steel Corporation was practically unknown at the time. He was merely Andrew Carnegie's office assistant until he gave birth to his famous IDEA. After that, he quickly rose to a position of power, fame, and riches.

CHAPTER 3

AUTO SUGGESTION

THE MEDIUM FOR INFLUENCING THE SUBCONSCIOUS MIND

THERE ARE NO LIMITATIONS TO THE MIND EXCEPT THOSE WE *ACKNOWLEDGE*

AUTO-SUGGESTION IS a term which applies to all suggestions and all self-administered stimuli which reach the mind through the five senses. Stated in another way, auto-suggestion is self-suggestion. It is the agency of communication between that part of the mind where conscious thought takes place, and that which serves as the seat of action for the subconscious mind. Through the dominating thoughts which one *permits* to remain in the conscious mind, (whether these thoughts be negative or positive, is immaterial), the principle of auto-suggestion voluntarily reaches the subconscious mind and influences it with these thoughts.

NO THOUGHT, whether it be negative or positive, CAN ENTER THE SUBCONSCIOUS MIND WITHOUT THE AID OF THE PRINCIPLE OF AUTO-SUGGESTION, with the exception of thoughts picked up from the ether. Stated differently, all sense impressions, perceived through the five senses, are stopped by the CONSCIOUS thinking mind, and may either be passed on to the subconscious mind, or rejected, at will. The conscious faculty serves, therefore, as an outer-guard to the approach of the subconscious.

Nature has built us to have ABSOLUTE CONTROL over the material which reaches the subconscious mind, through our five senses, although this is not meant to be construed as a statement that we always EXERCISE this control. In the great majority of instances, we do NOT exercise it, which explains why so many people go through life in poverty. Recall what has been said about the subconscious mind resembling a fertile garden spot, in which weeds will grow in abundance, if the seeds of more desirable crops are not planted. AUTO-SUGGESTION is the agency of control through which we can voluntarily feed the subconscious mind on thoughts of a creative nature, or, by neglect, permit thoughts of a destructive nature to find their way into this rich garden of the mind.

You were instructed, in the last of the six steps described in the chapter on Desire, to read ALOUD twice daily the WRITTEN statement of your DESIRE FOR MONEY, and to SEE AND FEEL yourself ALREADY in possession of the money! By following these instructions, you communicate the object of your DESIRE directly to your SUBCONSCIOUS mind in a spirit of absolute FAITH. Through repetition of this procedure, you voluntarily create thought habits favorable to your efforts to transform desire into its monetary equivalent. Go back to these six steps described in chapter two, and read them again, very carefully, before you proceed further. Then (when you come to it), read very carefully the four instructions for the organization of your "Master Mind" group, described in the chapter on Organized Planning. By comparing these two sets of instructions with what you just learned here, you will see that the instructions involve the application of auto-suggestion.

Remember, therefore, when reading aloud the statement of your desire (through which you are endeavoring to develop a "money consciousness"), that the mere reading of the words is of NO CONSEQUENCE, UNLESS you mix emotion or feeling with your words. If you repeat a million times the famous Emil Coué formula, "Day by day, in every way, I am getting better and better," without mixing emotion and FAITH with your words, you will experience no desirable results. Your subconscious mind recognizes and acts ONLY on thoughts well-mixed with emotion or feeling.

This is a fact of such importance as to warrant repetition in practically every chapter, because this lack of understanding is the main reason the majority of people who try to apply the principle of auto-suggestion get no desirable results.

Plain, unemotional words do not influence the subconscious mind. You will get no appreciable results until you learn to reach your subconscious mind with thoughts, or spoken words that have been well emotionalized with BELIEF.

Do not become discouraged, if you cannot control and direct your emotions the first time. Remember, there is no such thing as SOMETHING FOR NOTHING. Ability to reach and influence your subconscious mind has its price and you MUST PAY THAT PRICE. You cannot cheat, even if you want to. The price of ability to influence your subconscious mind is everlasting PERSISTENCE in applying the principles described here. You cannot develop the desired ability for a lower price. You, and YOU ALONE, must decide whether or not the reward for which you are striving (the "money consciousness"), is worth the price you must pay for it in effort.

Wisdom and "cleverness" alone, will not attract and retain money except in a few very rare instances, where the law of averages favors the attraction of money through these sources. The method of attracting money described here, does not depend upon the law of averages. In fact, the method plays no favorites. It will work for one person as effectively as it will for another. Where failure is experienced, it is the individual, *not the method*, which has failed. If you try and fail, make another effort, and still another, until you succeed.

Your ability to use the principle of auto-suggestion will depend, very largely, on your capacity to CONCENTRATE on a given DESIRE until that desire becomes a BURNING OBSESSION.

When you begin to carry out the instructions in connection with the six steps described in the second chapter, it will be necessary for you to make use of the principle of CONCENTRATION.

HOW TO CONCENTRATE

When you begin to carry out the first of the six steps, which instructs you to "fix in your own mind the EXACT amount of money you desire," hold your thoughts on that amount of money by CONCENTRATION, or fixation of attention, with your eyes closed, until you can ACTUALLY SEE the physical appearance of the money. Do this at least once each day. As you go through these exercises, follow the instructions given in the chapter on FAITH, and see yourself actually IN POSSESSION OF THE MONEY!

Important fact: the subconscious mind takes any orders given it in a spirit of absolute FAITH, and acts on those orders, although the orders often have to be presented over and over again, through repetition, before they are interpreted by the subconscious. Following the preceding statement, consider the possibility of playing a perfectly legitimate "trick" on your subconscious mind, by making it believe, *because you believe it*, that you must have the amount of money you are visualizing, that this money is already awaiting your claim, that the subconscious mind MUST hand over to you practical plans for acquiring the money which is yours. Hand over the thought suggested in the preceding paragraph to your IMAGINATION, and see what your imagination can, or will do, to create practical plans for the accumulation of money through transformation of your desire.

DO NOT WAIT for a definite plan, through which you intend to exchange services or merchandise in return for the money you are visualizing, but begin at once to see yourself in possession of the money, DEMANDING and EXPECTING, meanwhile, that your subconscious mind will hand over the plan, or plans you need. Be on the alert for these plans, and when they appear, put them into ACTION IMMEDIATELY. When the plans appear, they will probably "flash" into your mind through the sixth sense, in the form of an inspiration. This inspiration may be considered a direct communication, or message, from Infinite Intelligence. Treat it with respect, and act on it as soon as you receive it. Failure to do this will be FATAL to your success.

In the fourth of the six steps, you were instructed to "Create a definite plan for carrying out your desire, and begin at once to put this plan into action." You should follow this instruction in the manner described in the preceding paragraph. Do not trust to your "reason" when creating your plan for accumulating money through the transmutation of desire. Your reason is faulty. Moreover, your reasoning faculty may be lazy, and, if you depend on it entirely, it may disappoint you.

When visualizing the money you intend to accumulate, (with closed eyes), *see yourself rendering the service, or delivering the merchandise you intend to give in return for this money. This is important!*

SUMMARY OF INSTRUCTIONS

The fact that you are reading this book is an indication that you earnestly seek knowledge. It is also an indication that you are a student of this subject. If you are only a student, there is a chance that you may learn much that you did not know, but you will learn only by assuming an attitude of humility. If you choose to follow some of the instructions but neglect, or refuse to follow others—*you will fail!* To get satisfactory results, you must follow ALL instructions in a spirit of FAITH.

On the next page, the instructions given in connection with the six steps in the second chapter are summarized and blended with the principles covered by this chapter.

FOCUSED CONCENTRATION

First. Go into some quiet spot (preferably in bed at night) where you will not be disturbed or interrupted, close your eyes, and repeat aloud, (so you will hear your own words) the written statement of the amount of money you intend to accumulate, the time limit for its accumulation, and a description of the service or merchandise you intend to give in return for the money. As you speak, SEE YOURSELF ALREADY IN POSSESSION OF THE MONEY.

For example, suppose that you intend to accumulate $500,000 by the first of January, five years from now, that you intend to give personal services in return for the money, working in sales. Your written statement of your purpose should be similar to the following:

By the first day of January, 20___, I will have in my possession $_____, which will come to me in various amounts from time to time during the course of the next five years. In return for this money, I will give the most efficient service of which I am capable, rendering the fullest possible quantity and the best possible quality of service in the sale of . . . . (describe the service or merchandise you intend to sell).

I believe that I will have this money in my possession. My faith is so strong that I can now see this money before my eyes. I can touch it with my hands. It is awaiting transfer to me at the time and in the proportion that I deliver the service that I intend to provide in return for it. I am waiting for a plan to accumulate this money, and I will follow that plan, when I receive it.

Second. Repeat this program night and morning until you can see, (in your imagination) the money you intend to accumulate.

Third. Place a written copy of your statement where you can see it night and morning, and read it just before retiring, and upon arising until it has been memorized.

Remember, as you carry out these instructions, that you are applying the principle of auto-suggestion, giving orders to your subconscious mind. Remember, also, that your subconscious mind will act ONLY on instructions that are emotionalized, and handed over to it with "feeling." FAITH is the strongest and most productive of the emotions. Follow the instructions in the chapter on FAITH. They may seem abstract. Do not let this disturb you. Follow the instructions, no matter how abstract or impractical they may, at first, appear. The time will come, if you do as you have been instructed, *in spirit as well as in act*, when a new universe of power will unfold to you.

Skepticism, in connection with ALL new ideas, is characteristic of all human beings. But if you follow the instructions outlined, your skepticism will soon be replaced by belief, and this, in turn, will soon become crystallized into ABSOLUTE FAITH. Then you will have arrived at the point where you can truly say, "I am the master of my fate, I am the captain of my soul!" Many philosophers have made the statement, that we are the masters of our own *earthly* destinies, but most of them have failed to say *why*. The reason we are the masters of our own earthly status, and especially our financial status, is thoroughly explained in this chapter. You can become the master of yourself, and of your environment, because you have the POWER TO INFLUENCE YOUR OWN SUBCONSCIOUS MIND, and through it, gain the cooperation of Infinite Intelligence.

This chapter represents the keystone to the arch of this philosophy. The instructions in this chapter must be understood and APPLIED WITH PERSISTENCE, if you want to succeed in transforming desire into money. The actual performance of transforming DESIRE into money uses auto-suggestion as a way to reach and influence the subconscious mind. The other principles are simply tools with which to apply auto-suggestion. Keep this in mind, and you will be conscious of the important part auto-suggestion plays in your efforts to accumulate money through the methods described in this book. Carry out these instructions as though you were a child. Inject into your efforts something of the FAITH of a child. No impractical or unnecessary instructions have included been included here.

After you have read the entire book, come back to this chapter, and follow in spirit, and in action, this instruction:

READ THE ENTIRE CHAPTER ALOUD ONCE EVERY NIGHT, UNTIL YOU BECOME THOROUGHLY CONVINCED THAT THE PRINCIPLE OF AUTO-SUGGESTION IS EFFECTIVE, THAT IT WILL ACCOMPLISH FOR YOU ALL THAT HAS BEEN CLAIMED FOR IT. AS YOU READ, *UNDERLINE* EVERY SENTENCE THAT SPEAKS TO YOU.

Follow those instructions to the letter, and it will open the way for a complete understanding and mastery of the principles of success.

CHAPTER 4

SPECIALIZED KNOWLEDGE

SPECIALIZED KNOWLEDGE, PERSONAL EXPERIENCES, OR OBSERVATIONS

THERE ARE TWO kinds of knowledge. One is general, the other is specialized. General knowledge, no matter how great in quantity or variety it may be, is of little use in the accumulation of money. The faculties of the great universities possess practically every form of general knowledge known to civilization. *Most of the professors have very little or no money.* They specialize on *teaching* knowledge, but they do not specialize on the organization, or the *use* of knowledge. KNOWLEDGE will not attract money, unless it is organized and intelligently directed, through practical PLANS OF ACTION, to the DEFINITE END of accumulation of money. Lack of understanding of this fact has been the source of confusion to millions of people who falsely believe that "knowledge is power." It is nothing of the sort! Knowledge is only *potential* power. It becomes power only when, and if, it is organized into definite plans of action, and directed to a definite end. This "missing link" in all systems of education known to civilization today, may be found in the failure of educational institutions to teach their students HOW TO ORGANIZE AND USE KNOWLEDGE AFTER THEY ACQUIRE IT.

Many people make the mistake of assuming that, because Henry Ford had very little "schooling," he was not a man of "education." Those who make this mistake did not know Henry Ford, nor do they understand the real meaning of the word "educate." That word is derived from the Latin word "educo," meaning to educe, to draw out, to DEVELOP FROM WITHIN. An educated person is not, necessarily, one who has an abundance of general or specialized knowledge. An educated person is one who has so developed the faculties of mind that they can acquire anything they want, or its equivalent, without violating the rights of others. Henry Ford comes well within the meaning of this definition.

During the world war, a Chicago newspaper published certain editorials in which Henry Ford was called "an ignorant pacifist." Mr. Ford objected to the statements, and brought suit against the paper for libeling him. When the suit was tried in the Courts, the attorneys for the paper pleaded justification, and placed Mr. Ford, himself, on the witness stand, to prove to the jury that he was ignorant. The attorneys asked Mr. Ford a great variety of questions, all of them intended to prove, by his own evidence, that, while he might possess considerable specialized knowledge pertaining to the manufacture of automobiles, he was, in the main, ignorant.

Mr. Ford was plied with such questions as, "Who was Benedict Arnold?" and "How many soldiers did the British send over to America to put down the Rebellion of 1776?" In answer to the last question, Mr. Ford replied, "I do not know the exact number of soldiers the British sent over, but I have heard that it was a considerably larger number than ever went back."

Finally, Mr. Ford became tired of this line of questioning, and in reply to a particularly offensive question, he leaned over, pointed his finger at the lawyer who had asked the question, and said, "If I should really WANT to answer the foolish question you have just asked, or any of the other questions you have been asking me, let me remind you that I have a row of electric push-buttons on my desk, and by pushing the right button, I can summon to my aid men who can answer ANY question I desire to ask concerning the business to which I am devoting most of my efforts. Now, will you kindly tell me, WHY I should clutter up my mind with general knowledge, for the purpose of being able to answer questions, when I have men around me who can supply any knowledge I require?"

There certainly was good logic to that reply.

That answer floored the lawyer. Every person in the courtroom realized it was the answer, not of an ignorant man, but of a man of EDUCATION. Through the assistance of his "Master Mind" group, Henry Ford had at his command all the specialized knowledge he needed to enable him to become one of the wealthiest men in America. *It was not essential that he have this knowledge in his own mind.* Surely, no person who has sufficient inclination and intelligence to read a book of this nature can possibly miss the significance of this illustration.

Before you can be sure of your ability to transform DESIRE into its monetary equivalent, you will require SPECIALIZED KNOWLEDGE of the service, merchandise, or profession you intend to offer in return for fortune. Perhaps you need much more specialized knowledge than you have the ability or the inclination to acquire, and if this should be true, you may bridge your weakness through the aid of your "Master Mind" group. Andrew Carnegie stated that he, personally, knew nothing about the technical end of the steel business; moreover, he did not particularly care to know anything about it. The specialized knowledge he required for the manufacture and marketing of steel, he found available through the individual units of his MASTER MIND GROUP.

The accumulation of a great fortune calls for POWER, and power is acquired through highly organized and intelligently directed specialized knowledge, but that knowledge does not, necessarily, have to belong to the person who accumulates the fortune. Some people go through life with "inferiority complexes," because they are not "educated." Those who can organize and direct a "Master Mind" group of people who possess knowledge useful in the accumulation of money, is just as educated as anyone in the group. Thomas A. Edison had only three months of "schooling" during his entire life. He did not lack education, neither did he die poor. Henry Ford had less than a sixth grade "schooling" but he managed to do pretty well by himself, financially. Bill Gates had only two years of college education, but he managed to change the world, as we knew it, and became the richest man on earth.

SPECIALIZED KNOWLEDGE is among the most plentiful and cheapest forms of service around! If you doubt this, consult the payroll of any university. IT PAYS TO KNOW HOW TO PURCHASE KNOWLEDGE First of all, decide the sort of specialized knowledge you require, and the purpose for which it is needed. To a large extent, your major purpose in life, the goal toward which you are working, will help determine what knowledge you need. With this question settled, your next move requires that you have accurate information concerning dependable sources of knowledge. The more important of these are:

- Your own experience and education
- Experience and education available through cooperation of others (Master Mind Alliance)
- Colleges and Universities
- Information Databases and Libraries (Available online through books and periodicals, which contain all the knowledge that has ever existed in the world)
- Special Training Courses (through classes and home study)

As knowledge is acquired, it must be organized and put into use, for a definite purpose, through practical plans. Knowledge has no value except that which can be gained from its application toward some worthy end. This is one reason why college degrees are not valued more highly. They represent nothing but miscellaneous knowledge. If you contemplate taking additional schooling, first determine what you plan to do with that knowledge, and then learn where this particular sort of knowledge can be obtained. Successful people, in all callings, never stop acquiring specialized knowledge related to their major purpose, business, or profession. Those who are not successful usually make the mistake of believing that the knowledge acquiring period ends when one finishes school. The truth is that schooling does little more than to put one in the way of learning how to acquire practical knowledge. With this Changed World, which began with the economic collapse, came also astounding changes in educational requirements. The order of the day is COMPUTER LITERACY, LEADERSHIP, INSPIRATION, AND ADAPTABILITY!

This truth was emphasized by Randall Hansen and Katherine Hansen, founder and director of Quintessential Careers in the box on the next page.

Night classes offered in most major cities are one of the most reliable and practical sources of knowledge available to those who need schooling for use of specific software programs or other specific knowledge. Online and correspondence schools give specialized training anywhere in the world, on all subjects that can be taught by the extension method. One advantage of home study training is the flexibility of the program, which permits one to study during spare time. Another stupendous advantage of home study (if the school is carefully chosen), is that most courses offered by home study schools carry with them generous privileges of consultation which can be of priceless value to those needing specialized knowledge.

Anything acquired without effort, and without cost is generally unappreciated. The SELF-DISCIPLINE one receives from a definite program of specialized study makes up to some extent, for the wasted opportunity when knowledge was available without cost. Correspondence schools are highly organized business institutions. Their tuition fees are so low that they are forced to insist on prompt payments. Being asked to pay, whether the student makes good grades or not, has the effect of causing one to follow through with the course they otherwise drop. Online schools have not stressed this point sufficiently, for the truth is that their collection departments constitute the very finest sort of training on DECISION, PROMPTNESS, ACTION, and THE HABIT OF FINISHING WHAT WE START.

I learned this from experience, more than twenty-five years ago. I enrolled for a home study course in Advertising. After completing eight or ten lessons, I stopped studying, but the school did not stop sending me bills. I decided that if I had to pay for the course (which I had legally obligated myself to do), I should complete the lessons and get my money's worth. I felt, at the time, that the collection system of the school was somewhat too well organized, but I learned later in life that it was a valuable part of my training. Being forced to pay, I went ahead and completed the course. Later in life, I discovered that the efficient collection system of that school had been worth much in the form of money earned, because of the training in advertising I had gained.

SKILLS MOST SOUGHT AFTER BY EMPLOYERS:

Communications Skills. By far, the one skill mentioned most often by employers is the ability to listen, write, and speak effectively. Successful communication is critical in business.

Analytical/Research Skills. Deals with your ability to assess a situation, seek multiple perspectives, gather more information if necessary, and identify key issues that need to be addressed.

Computer/Technical Literacy. Almost all jobs now require some basic understanding of computer hardware and software, especially word processing, spreadsheets, and email.

Flexibility/Adaptability/Managing Multiple Priorities. Deals with your ability to manage multiple assignments and tasks, set priorities, and adapt to changing conditions and work assignments.

Interpersonal Abilities. The ability to relate to co-workers, inspire others to participate, and mitigate conflict with co-workers is essential given the amount of time spent at work each day.

Leadership/Management Skills. While there is some debate about whether leadership is something people are born with, these skills deal with your ability to take charge and manage your co-workers.

Planning/Organizing. Deals with your ability to design, plan, organize, and implement projects and tasks within an allotted timeframe. Also involves goal-setting.

We have in this country what is said to be the greatest public school system in the world. We have invested fabulous sums for fine buildings, we have provided convenient transportation for children living in the rural districts, so they may attend the best schools, but there is one astounding weakness to this marvelous system; IT IS FREE! One of the strange things about human beings is that they value only that which has a price. The free schools of America and the free public libraries do not impress people *because they are free*. This is the major reason why so many people find it necessary to acquire additional training after they quit school and go to work. It is also one of the major reasons why EMPLOYERS GIVE GREATER CONSIDERATION TO EMPLOYEES WHO PAY FOR SOME FORM OF EDUCATION. They have learned, from experience, that any person who has the ambition to give up their spare time to study at home, has leadership qualities. This recognition is not a charitable gesture, it is sound business judgment on the part of the employers.

There is one weakness in people for which there is no remedy. It is the universal weakness of LACK OF AMBITION! People, especially salaried people, who schedule their spare time, to provide for home study, seldom remain at the bottom very long. Their action opens the way for the upward climb, removes many obstacles from their path, and gains the friendly interest of those who have the power to put them in the way of OPPORTUNITY. The home study method of training is especially suited to the needs of employed people who find, after leaving school, that they must acquire additional knowledge, but don't have time to go back to school.

The changed economic conditions have made it necessary for thousands of people to find additional or new sources of income. The majority of these people will need to learn new technology or become more specialized. Many will be forced to change their occupations entirely. When a distributor finds that a certain line of merchandise is not selling, they usually replace it with one that is. If your services or skills do not bring adequate returns in one occupation, change to another where broader opportunities are available.

Stuart Austin Wier prepared himself as a Construction Engineer and followed this line of work until the great depression of the 1930s limited his market to where it did not give him the income he required. He took inventory of himself, decided to change his profession to law, went back to school, and took special courses to become a corporation lawyer. Despite the fact the depression had not ended, he completed his training, passed the Bar Exam, and quickly built a lucrative law practice in Dallas, Texas. Just to keep the record straight, and to anticipate the excuses of those who will say, "I couldn't go to school because I have a family to support," or "I'm too old," I will add the information that Mr. Wier was past forty and married when he went back to school. Moreover, by carefully selecting highly specialized courses, Mr. Wier completed in two years the work for which the majority of law students require four years. IT PAYS TO KNOW HOW TO PURCHASE KNOWLEDGE!

People who stop studying merely because they have finished school are forever hopelessly doomed to mediocrity, no matter what may be their calling. The way of success is the way of continuous pursuit of knowledge. Let us consider another example of prosperity during economic turmoil. During the great depression, a salesman in a grocery store found himself without a job. Having had some bookkeeping experience, he took a course in accounting, familiarized himself with all the latest bookkeeping and office equipment, and went into business for himself. Starting with the grocer for whom he had formerly worked, he made contracts with more than 100 small merchants to keep their books, at a very nominal monthly fee. His idea was so practical that he soon found it necessary to set up a portable office in a light delivery truck, which he equipped with all of his bookkeeping needs. He went on to develop a fleet of these bookkeeping offices "on wheels" and employed a large staff of assistants, providing small merchants with high quality accounting service, at a very nominal cost.

Specialized knowledge plus imagination were the ingredients that went into this unique and successful business, even during the great depression. The beginning of this successful business was an IDEA!

STARTING AT THE MIDDLE

The idea of starting at the bottom and working one's way up may appear to be sound, but the major objection to it is this: too many of those who begin at the bottom never manage to lift their heads high enough to be seen by OPPORTUNITY, so they remain at the bottom. It should be remembered, also, that the outlook from the bottom is not so very bright or encouraging. It has a tendency to kill off ambition. We call it "getting into a rut," which means that we accept our fate because we form the HABIT of daily routine, a habit that finally becomes so strong we cease to try to throw it off. And that is another reason why it pays to start one or two steps above the bottom. By doing so, one forms the HABIT of looking around, of observing how others get ahead, of seeing OPPORTUNITY, and of embracing it without hesitation.

Dan Halpin is a splendid example of what I mean. During his college days, he was manager of the famous National Championship Notre Dame football team, when it was under the direction of the late Knute Rockne.

Perhaps he was inspired by the great football coach to aim high, and NOT MISTAKE TEMPORARY DEFEAT FOR FAILURE, just as Andrew Carnegie, the great industrial leader, inspired his young business lieutenants to set high goals for themselves. At any rate, young Halpin finished college at a very unfavorable time, when the great depression had made jobs scarce. So, after a fling at investment banking and motion pictures, he took the first opening with a potential future he could find—selling electrical hearing aids on a commission basis. ANYONE COULD START IN THAT SORT OF JOB, AND HALPIN KNEW IT, but it was enough to open the door of opportunity to him.

For almost two years, he continued in a job not to his liking, and he would never have risen above that job if he had not done something about his dissatisfaction. He aimed, first, at the job of Assistant Sales Manager of his company, and got the job. That one step upward placed him high enough above the crowd to enable him to see still greater opportunity. It also placed him where OPPORTUNITY COULD SEE HIM. He did so well selling hearing aids, that the Chairman of the Board of a business competitor of the company for which Halpin worked, wanted to know something about that man Dan Halpin who was taking big sales away from their long established company. He sent for Halpin. When the interview was over, Halpin was the new Sales Manager, in charge of an entire division. Then, to test young Halpin's metal, Mr. Andrews went away to Florida for three months, leaving him to sink or swim in his new job. He did not sink! Knute Rockne's spirit of "All the world loves a winner, and has no time for a loser," inspired him to put so much into his job that he was elected Vice-President of the company, a job most people would be proud to earn after ten years of loyal effort. Halpin turned the trick in little more than six months.

It is difficult to say whether Mr. Andrews or Mr. Halpin is more deserving of praise, for the reason that both showed evidence of having an abundance of that very rare quality known as IMAGINATION. Mr. Andrews deserves credit for seeing, in young Halpin, a "go-getter" of the highest order. Halpin deserves credit for REFUSING TO COMPROMISE WITH LIFE BY ACCEPTING AND KEEPING A JOB HE DID NOT WANT, and that is one of the major points I am trying to emphasize through this entire philosophy—that we rise to high positions or remain at the bottom BECAUSE OF CONDITIONS WE CAN CONTROL IF WE DESIRE TO CONTROL THEM. I am also trying to emphasize another point, namely, that both success and failure are largely the results of HABIT! I have not the slightest doubt that Dan Halpin's close association with the greatest football coach America ever knew, planted in his mind the same brand of DESIRE to excel which made the Notre Dame football team world famous. Truly, there is something to the idea that hero-worship is helpful, provided one worships a WINNER. Halpin tells me that Rockne was one of the world's greatest leaders in history.

The bottom is a monotonous, dreary, unprofitable place for any person. That is why I have taken the time to describe how lowly beginnings may be circumvented by proper planning. The changed conditions ushered in by the world economic collapse has brought with it the need for newer and better ways of marketing PERSONAL SERVICES. No matter how bad the economy gets, people still have basic needs. They may not be purchasing yachts or new vacation homes, but they will still need their hair cut, suits dry-cleaned, and taxes done. More money changes hands in return for personal services than for any other purpose. The sum paid out monthly, to people who work for wages and salaries, is so huge that it runs into the billions. Perhaps some will find, in the IDEA here, the nucleus of the riches they DESIRE! Ideas are the seedlings from which great fortunes have grown.

Those seeing OPPORTUNITY lurking in this suggestion will find valuable aid in the chapter on Organized Planning. Incidentally, an efficient merchandiser of personal services will find demand for their services wherever people seek better markets for their services. By applying the Master Mind principle, a few people with suitable talent, could form an alliance, and have a paying business very quickly. One would need to be a fair writer, with a flair for advertising and selling, one handy at graphic design and copy, and one should be a first class business promoter who could let the world know about the service. If one person possessed all these abilities, they could carry the business alone, until it grew too big.

If you have the IMAGINATION, and seek a more profitable outlet for your personal services, this suggestion may be the stimulus for which you have been searching. The IDEA is capable of yielding an income far greater than that of the "average" doctor, lawyer, or engineer whose education required over a hundred thousand dollars and several years in college. The Idea is saleable to those seeking new positions, in practically all positions calling for managerial or executive ability, and those desiring re-arrangement of incomes in their present positions.

There is no fixed price for sound IDEAS!

Behind all IDEAS is specialized knowledge. Unfortunately, for those who do not find riches in abundance, specialized knowledge is more abundant and more easily acquired than IDEAS. Because of this very truth, there is a universal demand and an ever-increasing opportunity for the person capable of helping other people sell their personal services. Capability means IMAGINATION, the one quality needed to combine specialized knowledge with IDEAS, in the form of ORGANIZED PLANS designed to yield riches. If you have IMAGINATION, this chapter may present you with an idea sufficient to serve as the beginning of the riches you desire. Remember, the IDEA is the main thing. Specialized knowledge can be found just around the corner—any corner!

CHAPTER 5

IMAGINATION

THE WORKSHOP OF THE MIND

THE IMAGINATION IS literally the workshop that creates all of our plans. The impulse, the DESIRE, is given shape, form, and ACTION through the aid of the imaginative part of the brain. It has been said that we can create anything we can imagine. Of all periods in history, this is the most favorable for the development of the imagination, because it is an age of rapidly changing advancements and technology. Everywhere you look, you find things that stimulate and develop the imagination. Through imagination, we have discovered, and harnessed, more of nature's forces during the past hundred years than during the entire history of the human race. We have conquered the air so completely, that the birds are a poor match for us in flying. We have harnessed the ether, and made it serve as a means of instantaneous communication with any part of the world. We have analyzed, and weighed the sun at a distance of millions of miles, and determined, through the aid of IMAGINATION, the elements of which it consists. We have discovered that our own brain is both a broadcasting and receiving station for the vibration of thought, and we are beginning to learn how to make practical use of this discovery. We have increased the speed of computers and the internet, until we can retrieve information on any subject almost instantaneously.

OUR ONLY LIMITATION, within reason, LIES IN THE DEVELOPMENT AND USE OF IMAGINATION. We have not yet reached the apex of development in the use of our imaginative faculty. We have merely discovered that we have an imagination, and have used it in only very elementary ways.

TWO FORMS OF IMAGINATION

The imagination functions in two forms. One is known as "synthetic imagination," and the other as "creative imagination."

SYNTHETIC IMAGINATION

Through this faculty, we can arrange old concepts, ideas, or plans into new combinations. This faculty *creates* nothing. It merely works with the material of experience, education, and observation with which it is fed. It is the faculty used most by the inventor.

CREATIVE IMAGINATION

Through creative imagination, the finite mind has direct communication with Infinite Intelligence. It is this inherent power of the mind through which "hunches" and "inspirations" are received. It is by this power that all basic and new ideas are created and passed on. It is through the power of imagination that thought vibrations from the minds of others are received. It is through this power that one individual may "tune in," or communicate with the subconscious minds of others.

The creative imagination works automatically, in the manner described in subsequent pages. This power functions ONLY when the conscious mind is vibrating at an exceedingly rapid rate, for example, when the conscious mind is stimulated through the emotion of a *strong desire*. The creative ability becomes more alert, more receptive to vibrations from the sources mentioned, in proportion to its development through USE. This statement is significant! Ponder over it before passing on.

Keep in mind, as you follow these principles, that the entire story of how one converts DESIRE into money cannot be told in one statement. The story will be complete, only when one has MASTERED, ASSIMILATED, and BEGUN TO MAKE USE of all the principles. The great leaders of business, industry, finance, and the great artists, musicians, poets, and writers became great, because they developed the power of creative imagination. Both the synthetic and creative faculties of imagination become more alert with use, just as any muscle or organ of the body develops through use. Desire is only a thought, an impulse. It is nebulous and ephemeral. It is abstract and of no value until it has been transformed into its physical counterpart. While the synthetic imagination is the one used most frequently in the process of transforming the impulse of DESIRE into money, you must keep in mind that you may face circumstances and situations that demand use of the creative imagination as well.

Your imagination may have become weak through inaction. It can be revived and made alert through USE. This ability does not die, though it may become dormant through lack of use. Center your attention, for the time being, on the development of the synthetic imagination, because you will use it more often in the process of converting desire into money. Transformation of the intangible impulse, of DESIRE, into the tangible reality, of MONEY, calls for the use of a plan, or plans. These plans must be formed with the aid of the imagination, and mainly, with the synthetic faculty. Read the entire book through, then come back to this chapter, and begin at once to put your imagination to work on the building of a plan for transforming your DESIRE into money. Detailed instructions for the building of plans have been given in almost every chapter. Carry out the instructions best suited to your needs, reduce your plan to writing, if you haven't already. The moment you complete this, you will have DEFINITELY given concrete form to the intangible DESIRE. Read the preceding sentence once more. Read it aloud, very slowly, and as you do, remember that the moment you reduce the statement of your desire, and a plan for its realization, to writing, you have actually TAKEN THE FIRST of a series of steps, which will enable you to convert the thought into its physical counterpart.

The earth on which you live, you, yourself, and every other material thing are the result of evolutionary change, through which microscopic bits of matter have been organized and arranged in an orderly fashion. Moreover—and this statement is of stupendous importance—this earth, every one of the billions of individual cells of your body, and every atom of matter, *began as an intangible form of energy.* DESIRE is thought impulse! Thought impulses are forms of energy. When you begin with the thought impulse, DESIRE, to accumulate money, you are drafting into your service the same "stuff" that nature used in creating this earth and every material form in the universe, including the body and brain in which the thought impulses function.

As far as science has been able to determine, the entire universe consists of two primary elements—matter and energy. Everything we know has been created through the combination of energy and matter, from the largest star that floats in the heavens, down to human beings. You are now engaged in the task of trying to profit by nature's method. You are (sincerely and earnestly, we hope), trying to adapt yourself to nature's laws, by endeavoring to convert DESIRE into its physical or monetary equivalent. YOU CAN DO IT! IT HAS BEEN DONE BEFORE! You can build a fortune through the aid of laws which are immutable. But, first, you must become familiar with these laws, and learn to USE them. Through repetition, and by approaching the description of these principles from every conceivable angle, this book strives to reveal the secret to every great fortune. Strange and paradoxical as it may seem, the "secret" is NOT A SECRET. Nature, itself, advertises it in the earth, the stars, the planets suspended within our view, in the elements above and around us, in every blade of grass, and every form of life within our vision.

Nature advertises this "secret" in the terms of biology, in the conversion of a tiny cell, so small that it may be lost on the point of a pin, into the HUMAN BEING now reading this line. The conversion of desire into its physical equivalent is, certainly, no more miraculous! Do not become discouraged if you do not fully comprehend all that has been stated. Unless you have long been a student of the mind, it is not to be expected that you will assimilate all that is in this chapter on a first reading. But you will, in time, make good progress. The principles that follow will open the way for understanding imagination. Assimilate that which you understand, as you read this philosophy for the first time, then, when you reread and study it, you will discover that something has happened to clarify it, and give you a broader understanding of the whole. Above all, DO NOT STOP, nor hesitate in your study of these principles until you have read the book at least THREE times, for then, you will not want to stop.

PRACTICAL USE OF IMAGINATION

Ideas are the beginning points of all fortunes. Ideas are products of the imagination. Let us examine a few well known ideas that have yielded huge fortunes, with the hope to convey definite information concerning the method by which imagination may be used in accumulating riches.

THE ENCHANTED KETTLE

Over one-hundred years ago, an old country doctor drove to town, hitched his horse, quietly slipped into a drug store by the back door, and began "dickering" with the young drug clerk. His mission was destined to yield great wealth to many people. It was destined to bring to the South the most far-flung benefit since the Civil War. For more than an hour, behind the prescription counter, the old doctor and the clerk talked in low tones. Then the doctor left. He went out to the buggy and brought back a large, old fashioned kettle, a big wooden paddle (used for stirring the contents of the kettle), and deposited them in the back of the store.

The clerk inspected the kettle, reached into his inside pocket, took out a roll of bills, and handed it over to the doctor. The roll contained exactly $500.00, the clerk's entire savings. The doctor handed over a small slip of paper on which was written a secret formula. The words on that small slip of paper were worth a King's ransom! *But not to the doctor!* Those magic words were needed to start the kettle to boiling, but neither the doctor nor the young clerk knew what fabulous fortunes were destined to flow from that kettle.

The old doctor was glad to sell the outfit for five hundred dollars. The money would pay off his debts, and give him some peace of mind. The clerk was taking a big chance by staking his entire savings on a mere scrap of paper and an old kettle! He never dreamed his investment would start a kettle to overflowing with gold that would surpass the miraculous performance of Aladdin's lamp. What the clerk *really purchased* was an IDEA! The old kettle and the wooden paddle, and the secret message on a slip of paper were incidental. The strange performance of that kettle began to take place after the new owner mixed with the secret instructions an ingredient of which the doctor knew nothing.

Read this story carefully, give your imagination a test! See if you can discover what the young man added to the secret message that caused the kettle to overflow with gold. Remember, as you read, this is not a story from Arabian Nights. Here you have a story of facts, stranger than fiction, facts which began in the form of an IDEA.

Let us take a look at the vast fortunes of gold this idea has produced. It has paid, and still pays huge fortunes to people all over the world, who distribute the contents of the kettle to millions of people. The Old Kettle is now one of the world's largest consumers of sugar, thus providing jobs of a permanent nature to thousands of men and women engaged in growing sugar cane, and in refining and marketing sugar. The Old Kettle consumes, annually, millions of glass bottles, providing jobs to huge numbers of glass workers. The Old Kettle gives employment to an army of clerks, assistants, distributors, copy writers, and advertising experts throughout the nation. It has brought fame and fortune to scores of artists who have created magnificent pictures describing the product. The Old Kettle converted a small Southern city into the business capital of the South, where it now benefits, directly, or indirectly, every business and practically every resident of the city.

The influence of this idea now benefits every civilized country in the world, pouring out a continuous stream of gold to all who touch it. Gold from the kettle built and maintains one of the most prominent colleges of the South, where thousands of young people receive the training essential for success. The Old Kettle has done other marvelous things. All through the world depression, when factories, banks, and businesses were folding up by the thousands, the owner of this Enchanted Kettle went marching on, *giving continuous employment* to an army of men and women all over the world, and paying out extra portions of gold to those who, long ago, *had faith in the idea.*

If the product of that old brass kettle could talk, it would tell thrilling tales of romance in every language. Romances of love, romances of business, romances of professional men and women who are daily being stimulated by it. The first edition author is sure of at least one such romance, for he was a part of it, and it all began not far from the very spot on which the drug clerk purchased the old kettle. It was here that the author met his wife, and it was she who first told him of the Enchanted Kettle. It was the product of that Kettle they were drinking when he asked her to accept him "for better or worse."

Now that you know the content of the Enchanted Kettle is a world famous drink, it is fitting to know that the drink itself provides *stimulation of thought without intoxication*, and thereby it serves to give the refreshment of mind which many of us need to do our best work. Whoever you are, wherever you may live, whatever occupation you may be engaged in, just remember in the future, every time you see the words "Coca-Cola," that its vast empire of wealth and influence grew out of a single IDEA, and that the mysterious ingredient the drug clerk, Asa Candler, mixed with the secret formula was . . . IMAGINATION!

Stop and think of that, for a moment.

Remember, also, that the thirteen steps to riches, described in this book, were the media through which the influence of Coca-Cola has been extended to every city, town, village, and cross-roads of the world, and that ANY IDEA you may create, as *sound and meritorious* as Coca-Cola, has the possibility of duplicating the stupendous record of this world-wide thirst-killer. Truly, thoughts are things, and their scope of operation is the world, itself.

IF I HAD A MILLION DOLLARS

This story proves the truth of that old saying, "where there's a will, there's a way." It was told to me by that beloved educator and clergyman, the late Frank W. Gunsaulus, who began his preaching career in the stockyards region of South Chicago. While Dr. Gunsaulus was going through college, he observed many defects in our educational system, defects which he believed he could correct, if he were the head of a college. His *deepest desire* was to become the directing head of an educational institution in which young men and women would be taught to "learn by doing."

He made up his mind to organize a new college in which he could carry out his ideas, without being handicapped by orthodox methods of education. He needed a million dollars to put the project across! Where was he to lay his hands on, what was at the time, a very large a sum of money? That was the question that absorbed most of this ambitious young preacher's thought. But he couldn't seem to make any progress. Every night he took that thought to bed with him. He got up with it in the morning. He took it with him everywhere he went. He turned it over and over in his mind until it became a consuming *obsession* with him. A million dollars is a lot of money. He recognized that fact, but he also recognized the truth that *the only limitation is that which one sets up in one's own mind.*

Being a philosopher as well as a preacher, Dr. Gunsaulus recognized, as do all who succeed in life, that DEFINITENESS OF PURPOSE is the starting point from which one must begin. He recognized, too, that definiteness of purpose takes on animation, life, and power when backed by a BURNING DESIRE to translate that purpose into its material equivalent. He knew all these great truths, yet he did not know where, or how to lay his hands on a million dollars. The natural procedure would have been to give up and quit, by saying, "Ah well, my idea is a good one, but I cannot do anything with it, because I never can procure the necessary million dollars." That is exactly what the majority of people would have said, but it is not what Dr. Gunsaulus said. What he said, and what he did are so important that I will introduce him, and let him speak for himself:

One Saturday afternoon I sat in my room thinking of ways and means of raising the money to carry out my plans. For nearly two years, I had been thinking, but I had done nothing but think!

The time had come for ACTION!

I made up my mind, then and there, that I would get the necessary million dollars within a week. How? I was not concerned about that. The main thing of importance was the decision to get the money within a specified time, and I want to tell you that the moment I reached a definite decision to get the money within a specified time, a strange feeling of assurance came over me, such as I had never before experienced. Something inside me seemed to say, 'Why didn't you reach that decision a long time ago? The money was waiting for you the whole time!'

Things began to happen in a hurry. I called the newspapers and announced I would preach a sermon the following morning, entitled, 'What I would do if I had a Million Dollars.'

I went to work on the sermon immediately, but I must tell you, frankly, the task was not difficult, because I had been preparing that sermon for almost two years. The spirit behind it was a part of me!

Long before midnight I had finished writing the sermon. I went to bed and slept with a feeling of confidence, for I could see myself already in possession of the million dollars.

Next morning I arose early, went into the bathroom, read the sermon, then knelt on my knees and asked that my sermon might come to the attention of someone who would supply the needed money.

While I was praying I again had that feeling of assurance that the money would be forthcoming. In my excitement, I walked out without my sermon, and did not discover the oversight until I was in my pulpit and about ready to begin delivering it.

It was too late to go back for my notes, and what a blessing that I couldn't go back! Instead, my own subconscious mind yielded the material I needed. When I arose to begin my sermon, I closed my eyes, and spoke with all my heart and soul of my dreams. I not only talked to my audience, but I fancy I talked also to God. I told what I would do with a million dollars if that amount were placed in my hands. I described the plan I had in mind for organizing a great educational institution, where young people would learn to do practical things, and at the same time develop their minds.

When I had finished and sat down, a man slowly arose from his seat, about three rows from the rear, and made his way toward the pulpit. I wondered what he was going to do. He came into the pulpit, extended his hand, and said, 'Reverend, I liked your sermon. I believe you can do everything you said you would, if you had a million dollars. To prove that I believe in you and your sermon, if you will come to my office tomorrow morning, I will give you the million dollars. My name is Phillip D. Armour.'

Young Gunsaulus went to Mr. Armour's office and the million dollars was presented to him. With the money, he founded the Armour Institute of Technology. That is more money than the majority of preachers ever see in an entire lifetime, yet the thought impulse behind the money was created in the young preacher's mind in a fraction of a minute. The necessary million dollars came as a result of an idea. Behind the idea was a DESIRE that young Gunsaulus had been nursing in his mind for almost two years. Observe this important fact . . . HE GOT THE MONEY WITHIN THIRTY-SIX HOURS AFTER HE REACHED A DEFINITE DECISION IN HIS OWN MIND TO GET IT, AND DECIDED ON A DEFINITE PLAN FOR GETTING IT!

There was nothing new or unique about young Gunsaulus' vague thinking about a million dollars, and weakly hoping for it. Others before him, and many since his time, have had similar thoughts. But there was something very unique and different about the decision he reached on that memorable Saturday, when he put vagueness into the background, and definitely said, "I WILL get that money within a week!"

God seems to throw Himself on the side of those who know *exactly* what they want, *if they are determined* to get JUST THAT! Moreover, the principle through which Dr. Gunsaulus got his million dollars is still alive! It is available to you! This universal law is as workable today as it was when the young preacher made use of it so successfully. This book describes, step by step, the thirteen elements of this great law and suggests how they may be put to use. Observe that Asa Candler and Dr. Frank Gunsaulus had one characteristic in common: Both knew the astounding truth that IDEAS CAN BE TRANSFORMED INTO CASH THROUGH THE POWER OF DEFINITE PURPOSE, PLUS DEFINITE PLANS.

If you are one of those who believe that hard work and honesty, alone, will bring riches, destroy the thought! It is not true! Riches, when they come in huge quantities, are never the result of HARD work alone! Riches come, if they come at all, in response to definite demands, based on the application of definite principles, and not by chance or luck. Generally speaking, an idea is an impulse of thought that impels action, by an appeal to the imagination. All successful salespeople know that ideas can be sold where merchandise cannot. Ordinary salespeople do not know this—that is why they are ordinary.

A book publisher made a discovery that became invaluable to authors and publishers everywhere. He learned that people buy titles, and not contents, of books. By merely changing the name of one book that was not moving, sales on that book jumped upward more than a million copies. The inside of the book was not changed in any way. He merely replaced the cover bearing the title that did not sell, with a new cover and a title with "box-office" value.

That, as simple as it may seem, was an IDEA! It was IMAGINATION. There is no standard price on ideas. The creator of the idea sets the price, and, if well executed, they get it. The motion picture industry created a whole flock of millionaires. Most of them couldn't create ideas—BUT—they had the imagination to recognize ideas when they saw them. The next flock of millionaires grew out of the technology industry, which is still an industry of tremendous potential for any use of imagination. Money will be made by those who discover or create new and better forms of energy and technology.

The first wave of the internet was all about access to information. Companies like Google and Yahoo fundamentally changed the way we find and access all types of information. Where we were previously tied to print media for movie times, political events, and sports scores, we now can't imagine living without the internet. The second wave of the internet was focused on the social side of this information; how we shared information with each other. Sites like Facebook and Youtube have changed the way in which we share our lives, pictures, and videos with one another. We can now communicate with one another in real time updates, even when we are on opposite sides of the world. This second wave, Web 2.0, is struggling to cash in.

Though they have thousands of users and are known by every American, sites like LinkedIn and Twitter are not the powerhouses of profit they would like to be.

Here is a wide open field of opportunity screaming its protest at the way it is being butchered, because of lack of imagination, and begging for rescue at any price. Above all, the thing that Web 2.0 needs is new IDEAS! If this new field of opportunity intrigues you, perhaps you might profit by the suggestion that the successful networking sites of the future will give more attention to creating "buyer" audiences, much like what has happened with television and movies that advertise with product placement or create an entire market of products to be sold after a movie is released. Stated more plainly, the builder of networking sites who succeeds in the future must find practical ways to convert "socializers" into "buyers."

Advertisers are losing interest in buying banners and pop-ups. They want, and in the future will demand, indisputable proof that the social networking site on which they are advertising will generate the greatest number of sales possible. Another thing that might as well be understood by those who contemplate entering this field of opportunity, web advertising is going to be handled by an entirely new group of advertising experts, separate and distinct from the old time banner folks. The original cast in the online advertising game *don't get* the modern approach, because they have been schooled to SEE ideas. New techniques will demand people who can interpret ideas from a *written* banner in terms of *sound or motion.*

The internet, right now, is about where motion pictures were, when Mary Pickford and her curls first appeared on the screen. There is plenty of room for those who can *produce* or *recognize* IDEAS. If the comments on the opportunities of technology have not started your idea factory to work, you had better forget it. Your opportunity is in some other field. If the comment intrigued you in the slightest degree, then go further into it, and you may find the one IDEA you need to round out your career. Don't be discouraged you if you have no experience in technology. Andrew Carnegie knew very little about making steel, but he made practical use of two of the principles described in this book, and made the steel business yield him a fortune.

The story of practically every great fortune starts with the day when a creator of ideas and a seller of ideas got together and worked in harmony. Carnegie surrounded himself with people who could do all that he could not do: people who created ideas and people who put ideas into operation, and made himself and the others fabulously rich. Millions of people go through life hoping for favorable "breaks." Perhaps a favorable break can get one an opportunity, but the safest plan is not to depend on luck. It was a favorable "break" that gave me the biggest opportunity of my life, but twenty-five years of *determined effort* had to be devoted to that opportunity before it became an asset.

The "break" consisted of my good fortune in meeting and gaining the cooperation of Andrew Carnegie. On that occasion, Carnegie planted in my mind the *idea* of organizing the principles of achievement into a philosophy of success. Thousands of people have profited by the discoveries made in the twenty-five years of research, and several fortunes have been accumulated through the application of the philosophy. The beginning was simple. It was an IDEA that anyone could have developed. The favorable break came through Carnegie, but what about the DETERMINATION, DEFINITENESS OF PURPOSE, and the DESIRE TO ATTAIN THE GOAL, and the PERSISTENT EFFORT OF TWENTY-FIVE YEARS? It was no ordinary DESIRE that survived disappointment, discouragement, temporary defeat, criticism, and the constant reminding of "waste of time." It was a BURNING DESIRE! An OBSESSION!

When the idea was first planted in my mind by Mr. Carnegie, it was coaxed, nursed, and enticed to *remain alive*. Gradually, the idea became a giant under its own power, and it coaxed, nursed, and drove me. Ideas are like that. First, you give life, action, and guidance to ideas, and then they take on power of their own and sweep aside all opposition. Ideas are intangible forces, but they have more power than the physical brains that give birth to them. They have the power to live on, after the brain that creates them has returned to dust. For example, take the power of Christianity. That began with a simple idea, born in the brain of Christ. Its chief tenet was, "do unto others as you would have others do unto you." Christ has gone back to the source from where He came, but His IDEA goes marching on. Someday, it may grow up, and come into its own, then it will have fulfilled Christ's deepest DESIRE. The IDEA has been developing only two thousand years. Give it time!

CHAPTER 6

ORGANIZED PLANNING

THE CRYSTALLIZATION OF DESIRE INTO ACTION

YOU HAVE LEARNED that everything we create or acquire begins in the form of DESIRE and that desire is taken on the first lap of its journey, from the abstract to the concrete, into the workshop of the IMAGINATION, where PLANS for its transition are created and organized. In Chapter two, you were instructed to take six definite, practical steps, as your first move in translating the desire for money into its monetary equivalent. One of these steps is to form a DEFINITE, practical plan, or plans, through which this transformation may be made.

You will now be instructed how to build plans that will be practical, specifically:

- Ally yourself with a group of as many people as you need for the creation and carrying out of your plan for accumulating of money—making use of the "Master Mind" principle described in a later chapter. (Compliance with this instruction is absolutely essential. Do not neglect it.)

- Before forming your "Master Mind" alliance, decide what advantages and benefits, you may offer the individual members of your group in return for their cooperation. No one will work indefinitely without some form of compensation. No intelligent person will either request or expect another to work without adequate compensation, although this may not always be in the form of money.

- Arrange to meet with the members of your "Master Mind" group at least twice a week, and more often if possible, until you have jointly perfected the necessary plan.

- Maintain PERFECT HARMONY between yourself and every member of your "Master Mind" group. If you fail to carry out this instruction to the letter, expect to meet with failure. The "Master Mind" principle *cannot* work without PERFECT HARMONY.

KEEP IN MIND THESE FACTS

First. You are engaged in an undertaking of major importance to you. To be sure of success, you must have plans which are faultless.

Second. You must have the advantage of the experience, education, native ability and imagination of other minds. This is in harmony with the methods followed by every person who has accumulated a great fortune.

NO "I" IN TEAM

No individual has sufficient experience, education, native ability, and knowledge to insure the accumulation of a great fortune, without the cooperation of other people. Every plan you adopt, in your endeavor to accumulate wealth, should be the joint creation of yourself and every other member of your "Master Mind" group. You may originate your own plans, either In whole or in part, but SEE THAT THOSE PLANS ARE CHECKED AND APPROVED BY THE MEMBERS OF YOUR "MASTER MIND" ALLIANCE. If the first plan you adopt does not work successfully, replace it with a new plan; if this new plan fails to work, replace it, in turn with still another, and so on, until you find a plan that WORKS. Right here is the point where most people fail, because of their lack of PERSISTENCE in creating new plans to take the place of those that fail. The most intelligent person alive cannot succeed in accumulating money— or in any other undertaking—without plans which are practical and workable. Just keep this fact in mind, and remember when your plans fail, that temporary defeat is not permanent failure. It may only mean that your plans have not been sound. Build other plans. Start all over again.

Thomas A. Edison "failed" ten thousand times before he perfected the incandescent electric light bulb. That is—he met with *temporary defeat* ten thousand times, before his efforts were crowned with success. Temporary defeat should mean only one thing, the certain knowledge that there is something wrong with your plan. Millions of people go through life in misery and poverty, because they lack a sound plan through which to accumulate money. Henry Ford accumulated a fortune, not because of his superior mind, but because he adopted and followed a PLAN that proved to be sound. A thousand people could be pointed out, each with a better education than Ford's, yet each of whom lives in poverty, because they do not possess the RIGHT plan for accumulating money.

Your achievement can be no greater than your PLANS are sound. That may seem obvious, but it is true. Samuel Insull, the utility tycoon, lost his fortune of over one hundred million dollars. The Insull fortune was built on plans which were sound. The business depression forced Mr. Insull to CHANGE HIS PLANS; and the CHANGE brought "temporary defeat," because his new plans were NOT SOUND.

No one is ever whipped, until they QUIT—*in their own mind*. This fact will be repeated many times, because it is so easy to give up at the first sign of defeat. James J. Hill met with temporary defeat when he first endeavored to raise the necessary capital to build a railroad from the East to the West, but he, too, turned defeat into victory *through new plans*. Henry Ford met with temporary defeat, not only at the beginning of his automobile career, but after he had gone far toward the top. He created new plans, and went marching on to financial victory. We see people who have accumulated great fortunes, but we often recognize only their triumph, overlooking the temporary defeats which they had to surmount before "arriving." NO FOLLOWER OF THIS PHILOSOPHY CAN REASONABLY EXPECT TO ACCUMULATE A FORTUNE WITHOUT EXPERIENCING "TEMPORARY DEFEAT." When defeat comes, accept it as a signal that your plans are not sound; rebuild those plans and set sail once more toward your goal. If you give up before your goal has been reached, you are a "quitter." A QUITTER NEVER WINS AND A WINNER NEVER QUITS. Lift this sentence out, write it on a piece of paper in letters an inch high, and place it where you will see it every night before you go to sleep, and every morning before you go to work.

When you begin to select members for your "Master Mind" group, endeavor to select those who do not take defeat seriously. Some people foolishly believe that only MONEY can make money. This is not true! DESIRE, transformed into its monetary equivalent, through the principles laid down here, is how money is "made." Money, of itself, is nothing but inert matter. It cannot move, think, or talk, but it can "hear" when a person who DESIRES it, calls it to come!

DEVELOPING LEADERSHIP QUALITIES

The remainder of this chapter has been given over to a description of ways and means of becoming a great leader. The information here conveyed will be of priceless benefit to those who aspire to leadership in their chosen occupations. Intelligent planning is essential for success in any undertaking designed to accumulate riches. Broadly speaking, there are two types of people in the world. One type is known as LEADERS, and the other as FOLLOWERS. Decide at the outset whether you intend to become a leader in your chosen calling, or remain a follower. The difference in compensation is vast. The follower cannot reasonably expect the compensation to which a leader is entitled, although many followers make the mistake of expecting such pay.

It is no disgrace to be a follower. On the other hand, it is no credit to remain a follower. Most great leaders began in the capacity of followers. They became great leaders because they were INTELLIGENT FOLLOWERS. With few exceptions, those who cannot follow a leader intelligently cannot become effective leaders. Those who can follow a leader most efficiently are usually the people who develop into leadership most rapidly. An intelligent follower has many advantages, among them the OPPORTUNITY TO ACQUIRE KNOWLEDGE FROM A LEADER.

THE MAJOR ATTRIBUTES OF LEADERSHIP

- **UNWAVERING COURAGE** based on knowledge of self, and of one's occupation. No follower wishes to be dominated by a leader who lacks self-confidence and courage. No intelligent follower will be dominated by such a leader very long.
- **SELF-CONTROL.** People who cannot control themselves, can never control others. Self-control sets an example for one's followers that the more intelligent will emulate.
- **A KEEN SENSE OF JUSTICE.** Without a sense of fairness and justice, no leader can command and retain the respect of their followers.
- **DEFINITENESS OF PLANS.** The successful leader must plan the work, and *work the plan*. A leader who moves by guesswork, without practical, definite plans, is comparable to a ship without a rudder. Sooner or later it will land on the rocks.
- **THE HABIT OF DOING MORE THAN PAID FOR.** One of the penalties of leadership is the willingness, on the part of the leader, to do more than he or she requires of the followers.
- **A PLEASING PERSONALITY.** No slovenly, careless person can become a successful leader. Leadership calls for respect. Followers will not respect a leader who does not grade high on all of the factors of a Pleasing Personality.
- **DEFINITENESS OF DECISION.** People who waver in their decisions, show they are not sure of themselves. They cannot lead others successfully.
- **SYMPATHY AND UNDERSTANDING.** Successful leaders must be in sympathy with their followers. Moreover, they must understand them and their problems.
- **MASTERY OF DETAIL.** Successful leadership calls for mastery of details of the leader's position.
- **WILLINGNESS TO ASSUME FULL RESPONSIBILITY**. Successful leaders must be willing to assume responsibility for the mistakes and the shortcomings of their followers. If they try to shift this responsibility, he will not remain the leader. If a follower makes a mistake, and shows themselves incompetent, leaders must consider the failure their own.
- **COOPERATION.** Successful leaders must understand, and *apply* the principle of cooperative effort and be able to induce their followers to do the same. Leadership calls for POWER, and power calls for COOPERATION.

There are two forms of Leadership. The first, and by far the most effective, is LEADERSHIP BY CONSENT of the followers. The second is LEADERSHIP BY FORCE, without the consent and sympathy of the followers. History is filled with evidence that Leadership by Force does not last. The downfall and disappearance of most dictators and kings is significant. It means that people will not follow forced leadership indefinitely.

The world has just entered a new era of relationship between leaders and followers, which very clearly calls for new leaders and a new brand of leadership in business and industry. Those who belong to the old school of leadership-by-force, must acquire an understanding of the new brand of leadership (cooperation) or be relegated to the rank and file of the followers. There is no other way out for them. The relationship of employer and employee, or of leader and follower, in the future, will be one of mutual cooperation, based on an equitable division of the profits of business. In the future, the relationship of employer and employee will be more like a partnership than it has been in the past.

Napoleon, Kaiser Wilhelm of Germany, the Czar of Russia, and the King of Spain were examples of leadership by force. Their leadership disappeared. Without much difficulty, one might point to the prototypes of these ex-leaders, among the business, financial, and labor leaders of America who have been dethroned or slated to go. *Leadership-by-consent* of the followers is the only brand that can endure! People will follow forced leadership temporarily, but they will not do so willingly. The new brand of LEADERSHIP will embrace the eleven factors of leadership, described in this chapter, as well as some other factors. Those who make these the basis of their leadership, will find abundant opportunity to lead in any walk of life. The economic recovery has taken so long, largely, because the world lacks LEADERSHIP of the new brand. The demand for leaders who are competent in the new methods of leadership greatly exceeds the supply. Some of the old leaders will reform and adapt themselves to the new brand of leadership, but generally speaking, the world will have to look for new timber for its leadership.

This necessity may be your OPPORTUNITY!

THE MAJOR CAUSES OF FAILURE IN LEADERSHIP

We come now to the major faults of leaders who fail, because it is just as essential to know WHAT NOT TO DO as it is to know what to do.

- INABILITY TO ORGANIZE DETAILS. Efficient leadership calls for the ability to organize and master details. No genuine leader is ever "too busy" to do anything which may be required as the leader. When a person, whether a leader or follower, admits they are "too busy" to change plans, or to give attention to any emergency, they admit their inefficiency. The successful leader must be the master of all details connected with the position. That means, of course, they must learn to delegate details to capable lieutenants.

- UNWILLINGNESS TO PERFORM MUNDANE TASKS. Truly great leaders are willing, when occasion demands, to perform any work which they would ask another to perform. "The greatest among ye shall be the servant of all" is a truth which all able leaders observe and respect.

- EXPECTATION OF PAY FOR WHAT THEY "KNOW" INSTEAD OF WHAT THEY *DO* WITH WHAT THEY KNOW. The world does not pay people for what they "know." It pays them for what they DO, or induce others to do.

- FEAR OF COMPETITION FROM FOLLOWERS. Leaders who fear that a follower may take their position is practically sure make that fear a reality sooner or later. Able leaders train understudies to whom they can delegate, at will, any of the details of their job. Only in this way, can leaders multiply themselves and be at many places, and give attention to many things at one time. It is an eternal truth that people receive more pay for their ABILITY TO GET OTHERS TO PERFORM, than they could possibly earn by their own efforts. Efficient leaders, through knowledge of their jobs and the magnetism of their personalities, can greatly increase the efficiency of others, and induce them to work harder and better than they could without such leadership.

- LACK OF IMAGINATION. Without imagination, leaders are incapable of meeting emergencies, and of creating plans to guide their followers efficiently.

- SELFISHNESS. Leaders who take all the credit for the work of their followers are sure to be met with resentment. The really great leaders TAKE NO CREDIT. They are content to see the honors, when there are any, go to their followers, because they know that most people will work harder for recognition than they will for money alone.

- DISLOYALTY. Perhaps this should have come at the head of the list. Leaders who is not loyal to their followers, and to their associates, those above them, and those below them, cannot maintain a position of leadership. Disloyalty marks people as being less than the dust of the earth. Lack of loyalty is one of the major causes of failure in every walk of life.

- EMPHASIS OF THE "AUTHORITY" OF LEADERSHIP. Effective leaders leads by encouraging, and not by trying to instill fear in the hearts of their followers. Leaders who try to impress followers with their "authority" fall into the category of leadership through FORCE. REAL LEADERS, have no need to advertise that fact except by their conduct: their sympathy, understanding, fairness, and a demonstration that they know their job.

- EMPHASIS OF TITLE. Competent leaders require no "title" to give them the respect of their followers. People who make too much of their titles generally have little else to emphasize. The doors to the office of real leaders are open to all who wish to enter, and their working environments are free from formality or ostentation.

These are among the more common of the causes of failure in leadership. Any one of these faults is sufficient to induce failure. Study the list carefully if you aspire to leadership and make sure that you are free of these faults.

FIELDS IN NEED OF "NEW LEADERSHIP"

Before leaving this chapter, your attention is called to a few of the fertile fields in which there has been a decline of leadership, and in which the new type of leader may find an abundance of OPPORTUNITY.

First. In the field of politics there is a most insistent demand for new leaders; a demand which indicates nothing less than an emergency. The majority of politicians have, seemingly, become high-grade, legalized criminals. They have fallen so deeply into the pockets of special interest and have taken such liberties with tax dollars that the people can no longer stand the burden.

Second. The banking business is undergoing a reform. The leaders in this field have entirely lost the confidence of the public. Already the bankers have sensed the need of reform, and they have begun it.

Third. The business world calls for new leaders. The old leaders thought and moved in terms of dividends instead of thinking and moving in terms of human equations! Future leader in business must regard themselves as quasi-public officials whose duty it is to manage trust in such a way that it will burden no individual or group of individuals. Profit at the expense of others is a thing of the past. Let those who aspire to leadership in the field of business remember this.

Fourth. Religious leaders of the future will be forced to give more attention to the material needs of their followers, in findings solutions to their economic and personal problems of the present, and less attention to the past, and the yet unborn future.

Fifth. In the professions of law, medicine, and education, a new brand of leadership, and to some extent, new leaders will become a necessity. This is especially true in the field of education. Leaders in that field must, in the future, find ways and means of teaching people HOW TO APPLY the knowledge they receive in school. They must deal more with PRACTICE and less with THEORY.

Sixth. New leaders will be required in the field of journalism. Newspapers are soon to disappear, and reporting the news successfully will require a divorce from "special privilege" and content will be relieved from the influence of advertisers. Effective news outlets will cease to be organs of propaganda for special interests.

These are but a few of the fields in which opportunities for new leaders and a new brand of leadership are now available. The world is undergoing a rapid change. This means that the media, through which the changes in human habits are promoted, must be adapted to the changes. The media described here, are those that, more than any others, determine the trend of civilization.

GET THE JOB YOU WANT

Everyone enjoys doing the kind of work for which they are best suited. Artists love to work with paints, carpenters with their hands, writers love to write. Those with less definite talents have their preferences for certain fields. If America does anything well, it offers a full range of occupations, manufacturing, marketing, and the professions. Below are seven steps for getting the exact position you're seeking.

First. Decide EXACTLY what kind of a job you want. If the job doesn't already exist, perhaps you can create it.

Second. Choose the company, or individual for whom you wish to work.

Third. Study your prospective employer, as to policies, personnel, and chances of advancement.

Fourth. By analysis of yourself, your talents and capabilities, figure WHAT YOU CAN OFFER, and plan ways and means of giving advantages, services, developments, ideas that *you believe* you can successfully deliver.

Fifth. Forget about "a job." Forget whether or not there is an opening. Forget the usual routine. Concentrate on what *you can give*.

Sixth. Once you have your plan in mind, arrange with an experienced writer to put it on paper in neat form, and in full detail.

Seventh. Present it to the *proper person with authority* and they will do the rest. Every company is looking for people who can give something of value, whether it be ideas, services, or "connections." Every company has room for people with a definite plan of action which is to the advantage of that company.

This process may take a few days or weeks of extra time, but the difference in income, in advancement, and in gaining recognition will save years of hard work at small pay. It has many advantages, the main one being that it will often save you one to five years in reaching a chosen goal.

Every person who starts, or "gets in" half way up the ladder, does so by deliberate and careful planning.

COMMON CAUSES OF FAILURE

HOW MANY OF THESE ARE HOLDING YOU BACK?

Life's greatest tragedy consists of people who earnestly try, and fail! The tragedy lies in the overwhelmingly large majority of people who fail, as compared to the few who succeed. I have had the privilege of analyzing several thousand men and women, 98% of whom were classed as "failures." There is something radically wrong with a civilization, and a system of education, which permit 98% of the people to go through life as failures. But I did not write this book to moralize on the rights and wrongs of the world; that would require a book a hundred times the size of this one. My analysis work proved that there are thirty major reasons for failure, and thirteen major principles through which people accumulate fortunes.

In this chapter, a description of the thirty major causes of failure will be given. As you go over the list, check yourself by it, point by point, to discover how many of these causes-of-failure stand between you and success.

- UNFAVORABLE HEREDITARY BACKGROUND. There is little, if anything, that can be done for people born with a deficiency in brain power. This philosophy offers one method of bridging this weakness—through the aid of the Master Mind. Observe with profit, however, that this is the ONLY one of the thirty causes of failure that cannot be *easily corrected*.

- LACK OF A WELL-DEFINED PURPOSE IN LIFE. There is no hope of success for the person who does not have a central purpose, or *definite goal* at which to aim. Ninety-eight out of every hundred of those whom I have analyzed, had no such aim. Perhaps this was the MAJOR CAUSE OF THEIR FAILURE.

- LACK OF AMBITION TO AIM ABOVE MEDIOCRITY. We offer no hope for the person who is so indifferent as not to want to get ahead in life, and who is not willing to pay the price.

- INSUFFICIENT EDUCATION. This is a handicap that may be overcome more easily than others. Experience has proven that the best-educated people are often those who are "self-made," or self-educated. It takes more than a college degree to have education. Educated have learned to get what they want in life without violating the rights of others. Education consists, not so much of knowledge, but of knowledge effectively and persistently APPLIED. People are paid, not merely for what they know, but more particularly for WHAT THEY DO WITH WHAT THEY KNOW.

- UNFAVORABLE INFLUENCES DURING CHILDHOOD. "As the twig is bent, so shall the tree grow." Most people who have criminal tendencies acquire them as the result of bad environment, and improper associates during childhood.

- PROCRASTINATION. This is one of the most common causes of failure. Procrastination stands in the shadow of every human being, waiting for its opportunity to spoil the chances for success. Most of us go through life as failures, because we are waiting for the "time to be right" to start doing something worthwhile. Do not wait. The time will never be "just right." Start where you stand, and work with whatever tools you have at your command, and better tools will be found as you go along.

- LACK OF PERSISTENCE. Most of us are good "starters" but poor "finishers" of everything we begin. Moreover, people are prone to give up at the first signs of defeat. There is no substitute for PERSISTENCE. People who make PERSISTENCE their motto, discover that failure finally becomes tired, and makes its departure. Failure cannot cope with PERSISTENCE.

- NEGATIVE PERSONALITY. There is no hope of success for the person who repels people through a negative personality. Success comes through the application of POWER, and power is attained through the cooperative efforts of other people. A negative personality will not induce cooperation.

- UNCONTROLLED DESIRE FOR "SOMETHING FOR NOTHING." The gambling mentality drives millions of people to failure.

- LACK OF A WELL DEFINED POWER OF DECISION. People who succeed reach decisions promptly, and change them, if at all, very slowly. People who fail, reach decisions, if at all, very slowly, and change them frequently and quickly. Indecision and procrastination are twins. Where one is found, the other may usually be found also. Kill off this pair before they completely chain you to the treadmill of FAILURE.

- ONE OR MORE OF THE SIX BASIC FEARS. These fears will be analyzed in detail in a later chapter.

- WRONG SELECTION OF A PARTNER IN MARRIAGE. This a most common cause of failure. The relationship of marriage brings people intimately into contact. Unless this relationship is harmonious, failure is likely to follow. Moreover, it will be a form of failure that is marked by misery and unhappiness, destroying all signs of AMBITION.

- OVER-CAUTION. The person who takes no chances, generally has to take whatever is left when others are through choosing. Over-caution is as bad as under-caution. Both are extremes to be guarded against. Life itself is filled with the element of chance.

- WRONG SELECTION OF ASSOCIATES IN BUSINESS. This is one of the most common causes of failure in business. We emulate those with whom we associate most closely. Pick a business partner (or employer) who is worth emulating.

- SUPERSTITION AND PREJUDICE. Superstition is a form of fear. It is also a sign of ignorance. People who succeed keep open minds and are afraid of nothing.
- WRONG SELECTION OF A VOCATION. No one can succeed in a line of work they do not like. The most essential step in your success is selecting an occupation you can throw yourself into wholeheartedly.
- LACK OF CONCENTRATION OF EFFORT. The "jack-of-all-trades" seldom is good at any. Concentrate all of your efforts on one DEFINITE CHIEF AIM.
- THE HABIT OF INDISCRIMINATE SPENDING. Spend-thrifts cannot succeed, mainly because they stand eternally in FEAR OF POVERTY. Form the habit of systematic saving by putting aside a definite percentage of your income. Money in the bank gives one a very safe foundation of COURAGE when working. Without money, one must take what one is offered, and be glad to get it.
- LACK OF ENTHUSIASM. Without enthusiasm no one can be convincing. Moreover, enthusiasm is contagious, and the person who has it, under control, is generally welcome in any group of people.
- INTOLERANCE. The person with a "closed" mind on any subject seldom gets ahead. Intolerance means that one has stopped acquiring knowledge. The most damaging forms of intolerance are those connected with religious, racial, and political differences of opinion.
- INTEMPERANCE. The most damaging forms of intemperance are connected with drinking, drugs, and sexual activities. Overindulgence in any of these is fatal to success.
- INABILITY TO COOPERATE WITH OTHERS. More people lose their positions and their big opportunities in life, because of this fault, than for all other reasons combined. It is a fault which no well-informed business person or leader will tolerate.
- POSSESSION OF POWER THAT WAS NOT ACQUIRED THROUGH SELF EFFORT. (Sons and daughters of wealthy people, and others who inherit money they did not earn). Power in the hands of one who did not acquire it gradually, is often fatal to success. QUICK RICHES are more dangerous than poverty.
- INTENTIONAL DISHONESTY. There is no substitute for honesty. One may be temporarily dishonest by force of circumstances over which one has no control, without permanent damage. But, there is NO HOPE for the person who is dishonest by choice. Sooner or later, their deeds will catch up with them, and they will pay by loss of reputation and perhaps even loss of liberty.

- EGO AND VANITY. These qualities serve as red lights that warn others to keep away. THEY ARE FATAL TO SUCCESS.
- GUESSING INSTEAD OF THINKING. Most people are too indifferent or lazy to acquire FACTS with which to THINK ACCURATELY. They prefer to act on "opinions" created by guesswork or snap-judgments.
- LACK OF CAPITAL. This is a common cause of failure among those who start out in business for the first time, without sufficient reserve of capital to absorb the shock of their mistakes, and to carry them over until they have established a REPUTATION.

In these thirty major causes of failure is a description of the tragedy of life, which applies to practically every person who tries and fails. It will be helpful if you can ask someone who knows you well to go over this list with you, and help to analyze you by the thirty causes of failure. It may work on your own, but most people cannot see themselves as others see them. One of the oldest words of advice is "Know yourself!" If you market merchandise successfully, you must know the merchandise. The same is true in marketing yourself. You should know all of your weaknesses so that you can either bridge them or eliminate them. You should know your strengths so that you can call attention to them. You can know yourself only through *accurate* analysis.

The mistake of ignorance in connection with self was displayed by a young man who applied for a job with a well known company. He made a very good impression until the manager asked him what salary he expected. He replied that he had no fixed sum in mind (*lack of a definite aim*). The manager then said, "We will pay you all you are worth, after we try you out for a week."

"I will not accept it," the applicant replied, "because I AM GETTING MORE THAN THAT WHERE I AM NOW EMPLOYED."

Before you even start to negotiate for a readjustment of your salary in your present position, or to seek employment elsewhere, BE SURE THAT YOU ARE WORTH MORE THAN YOU NOW RECEIVE. It is one thing to WANT money—everyone wants more—but it is something entirely different to be WORTH MORE! Many people mistake their WANTS for their JUST DUES. Your financial requirements or wants have nothing to do with your WORTH. Your value is established entirely by your ability to contribute useful service or your capacity to induce others to contribute such service.

TAKE INVENTORY OF YOURSELF

Annual self-analysis is essential in the effective marketing of your abilities. Moreover, a yearly self-analysis should trend toward a DECREASE IN FAULTS, and an increase in VIRTUES. One goes ahead, stands still, or goes backward in life. The goal should be, of course, to move ahead. Annual self-analysis will show you if advancement has been made, and if so, how much. It will also disclose any backward steps you may have made. The effective marketing of yourself requires you to move forward even if the progress is slow.

Your annual self-analysis should be made at the end of each year, so you can include in your New Year's Resolutions any improvements that the analysis indicates should be made. Take this inventory by asking yourself the following questions, and by checking your answers with the aid of someone who will not permit you to deceive yourself as to their accuracy.

SELF-ANALYSIS QUESTIONNAIRE FOR PERSONAL INVENTORY

1. Have I attained the goals for this year? (You should work with a definite yearly objective to be attained as a part of your major life objective). YES /NO IF NO, HOW CAN I IMPROVE?

    _____

2. Have I delivered the best possible QUALITY service I was capable of, or could I have improved any part of this service? YES NO IF NO, HOW CAN I IMPROVE?

    _____

3. Have I delivered service in the greatest possible QUANTITY of which I was capable? YES /NO IF NO, HOW CAN I IMPROVE?

    _____

4. Has the spirit of my conduct been harmonious and cooperative at all times? YES /NO IF NO, HOW CAN I IMPROVE?

    _____

5. Have I permitted the habit of PROCRASTINATION to decrease my efficiency, and if so, to what extent? YES /NO IF NO, HOW CAN I IMPROVE?

    _____

6. Have I improved my PERSONALITY, and if so, in what ways? YES /NO IF NO, HOW CAN I IMPROVE?

    _____

7. Have I been PERSISTENT in following my plans through to completion? YES /NO IF NO, HOW CAN I IMPROVE?

    _____

THINK AND GROW RICH

8. Have I reached DECISIONS PROMPTLY AND DEFINITELY on all occasions? YES /NO IF NO, WHY NOT?

_____

9. Have I permitted any one or more of the six basic fears to decrease my effectiveness? YES /NO IF YES, WHICH ONE/S?

_____

10. Have I been either "over-cautious," or "under-cautious?" IF SO, WHY?

_____

11. Has my relationship with my co-workers been pleasant, or unpleasant? If it has been unpleasant, what role did I play? How did I contribute?

_____

12. Have I wasted energy through lack of CONCENTRATION of effort? YES /NO IF NO, HOW CAN I IMPROVE?

_____

13. Have I been open minded and tolerant in general? YES /NO IF NO, HOW CAN I IMPROVE?

_____

_____

14. In what way have I improved my abilities?

_____

15. Have I been indulgent or excessive in any of my bad habits? YES /NO IF YES, HOW DO I PLAN TO CHANGE IT?

_____

16. Have I expressed, either openly or secretly, any form of EGO? YES /NO IF YES, HOW CAN I IMPROVE?

_____

17. Has my conduct toward my co-workers led them to RESPECT me? YES /NO IF NO, HOW CAN I CHANGE THAT?

_____

18. Have my opinions and DECISIONS been based on guesswork, or accuracy of analysis and THOUGHT?

_____

19. Have I followed the habit of budgeting my time, my expenses, and my income, and have I been conservative in these budgets? YES /NO IF NO, WHAT AREAS NEED IMPROVEMENT?

_____

20. How much time have I devoted to UNPROFITABLE effort that I might have used to better advantage?

_____

21. How may I RE-BUDGET my time, and change my habits so I will be more effective during the coming year?

_____

22. Have I been guilty of any conduct that was not approved by my conscience? YES /NO IF YES, WHAT WAS IT?

_____

23. In what ways have I gone above and beyond the requirements of my job?

_____

24. Have I been unfair to anyone, and if so, in what way?

_____

25. If I had been the purchaser of my own services (my employer) for the year, would I be satisfied with my purchase? YES /NO IF NO, WHERE DO CHANGES NEED TO BE MADE?

_____

26. Am I in the right line of work, and if not, why not?

_____

27. Has the purchaser of my services (my employer and/or clients) been satisfied with the service I have rendered, and if not, why not?

_____

Having read and assimilated the information conveyed through this chapter, you are now ready to create a practical plan for marketing yourself. In this chapter are adequate descriptions of every principle essential in planning the marketing of yourself, including the major attributes of leadership; the most common causes of failure in leadership; a description of the fields of opportunity for leadership; the main causes of failure in all walks of life, and the questions that should be used in self-analysis.

This extensive and detailed presentation of accurate information has been included, because it will be needed by all who must begin the accumulation of riches by marketing themselves. Those who have lost their fortunes, and those who are just beginning to earn money, have nothing but personal services to offer in return for wealth. This chapter will be of great value to all who aspire to attain leadership in any calling. It will be particularly helpful to those aiming to market themselves as business or industrial executives. Complete assimilation and understanding of the information will be helpful in marketing one's own services, and it will also help one to become more analytical and capable of judging other people. The information will be priceless to personnel directors, employment managers, and other executives in charge of hiring and staffing, and the maintenance of efficient organizations.

FINDING OPPORTUNITIES FOR WEALTH

Now that we have analyzed the principles by which wealth may be accumulated, we naturally ask, "where do you find the opportunities to apply these principles?" Very well, let us take inventory and see what the United States of America offers the person seeking wealth, great or small. To begin, let us remember, *all of us*, that we live in a country where *every law-abiding citizen enjoys freedom of thought and freedom of action unequaled anywhere in the world*. Most of us have never taken inventory of the advantages of this freedom. We have never compared our unlimited freedom with the curtailed freedom in other countries. Here we have freedom of thought, freedom in the choice and enjoyment of education; freedom in religion, in politics, in the choice of a business, profession, or occupation; freedom to accumulate and own *ALL THE PROPERTY WE CAN ACCUMULATE*; freedom to choose our place of residence, freedom in marriage, freedom to all races; freedom of travel from one state to another, freedom in our choice of foods, and freedom to *AIM FOR ANY STATION IN LIFE FOR WHICH WE HAVE PREPARED OURSELVES*, even for the presidency of the United States. We have other forms of freedom, but this list will give a bird's eye view of the most important, which constitute OPPORTUNITY of the highest order. This advantage of freedom is all the more conspicuous because the United States is the only country guaranteeing to every citizen, whether native born or naturalized, so broad and varied a list of freedoms.

THE "MIRACLE" THAT HAS PROVIDED THESE BLESSINGS

We often hear politicians proclaiming the freedom of America, when they solicit votes, but seldom do they take the time or devote sufficient effort to the analysis of the source or nature of this "freedom." Having no axe to grind, no grudge to express, no ulterior motives to be carried out, I have the privilege of going into a frank analysis of that mysterious, abstract, greatly misunderstood "SOMETHING" which gives to every citizen of America more blessings, more opportunities to accumulate wealth, more freedom of every nature, than may be found in any other country. I have the right to analyze the source and nature of this UNSEEN POWER, because I know, and have known for more than a quarter of a century, many of the people who organized that power, and many who are now responsible for its maintenance.

The name of this mysterious benefactor of mankind is CAPITAL! CAPITAL consists not alone of money, but more particularly of highly organized, intelligent groups of people who plan ways and means of using money efficiently for the good of the public, and profitably for themselves. These groups consist of scientists, educators, chemists, inventors, business analysts, publicists, transportation experts, accountants, lawyers, doctors, and people with highly specialized knowledge in all fields. They pioneer, experiment, and blaze trails in new fields of endeavor. They support colleges, hospitals, public schools, build roads, publish newspapers, pay most of the cost of government, and take care of the multitude of details essential to human progress. Stated briefly, the capitalists are the brains of civilization, because they supply the entire fabric of which all education, enlightenment, and human progress consists.

Money, without brains, is always dangerous. Properly used, it is the most important element of civilization. A simple breakfast could not be delivered to a New York family, or any other family, if organized capital had not provided the machinery, the ships, the railroads, and the huge armies of trained employees to operate them. Some slight idea of the importance of ORGANIZED CAPITAL may be had by trying to imagine yourself burdened with the responsibility of collecting, without the aid of capital, and delivering to a New York City family, a simple breakfast. To supply the tea, you would have to make a trip to China or India, both a very long way from America. Unless you are an excellent swimmer, you would become rather tired before making the round trip. Then, too, another problem would confront you. What would you use for money, even if you had the physical endurance to swim the ocean? To supply the sugar, you would have to take a long hike to Brazil. But even then, you might come back without the sugar, because organized effort and money are necessary to produce sugar, to say nothing of what is required to refine, transport, and deliver it to the breakfast table anywhere in the United States.

The eggs, you could deliver easily enough from the barn yards near New York City, but you would have a very long walk to Florida and return, before you could serve the two glasses of grapefruit juice. You would have another long walk, to Kansas, or one of the other wheat growing states, when you went after the wheat bread for the toast. The cereal would have to be omitted from the menu, because it would not be available except through the labor of a trained staff and suitable machinery, ALL OF WHICH CALL FOR CAPITAL.

While resting, you could take off for another little swim down to South America, where you would pick up a couple of bananas, and on your return, you could take a short walk to the nearest farm having a dairy and pick up some butter and cream. Then your New York City family would be ready to sit down and enjoy breakfast, and *you could collect your two dimes for your labor!* Seems absurd, doesn't it? Well, the procedure described would be the only possible way these simple items of food could be delivered to the heart of New York City, if we had no capitalist system.

The sum of money required for the building and maintenance of the railroads and ships used in the delivery of that simple breakfast is so huge that it staggers the imagination. It runs into hundreds of millions of dollars, not to mention the armies of trained employees required to man the ships and trains. But, transportation is only a part of the requirements of modern civilization in capitalist America. Before there can be anything to haul, something must be grown from the ground or manufactured and prepared for market. This calls for hundreds of millions of dollars for equipment, machinery, boxing, marketing, and for the wages of millions of men and women.

Ships and railroads do not spring up from the earth and function automatically. They come in response to the call of civilization, through the labor and ingenuity and organizing ability of people who have IMAGINATION, FAITH, ENTHUSIASM, DECISION, and PERSISTENCE! These people are capitalists. They are motivated by the desire to build, construct, achieve, contribute, earn profits, and accumulate wealth. And, because they CONTRIBUTE TO THE EXISTENCE OF CIVILIZATION, they put themselves in the path of great wealth.

The purpose of this book—*A purpose to which I have devoted over a quarter of a century*—is to present to all who want the knowledge, the most dependable philosophy through which individuals may accumulate wealth in whatever quantity they desire. I have analyzed the economic advantages of the capitalist system for the purpose of showing that all who seek wealth must recognize and adapt themselves to the system that controls all approaches to fortunes, large or small. This is a capitalist country, it was developed through the use of capital, and we who claim the right to partake of the blessings of freedom and opportunity, we who seek to accumulate riches here, may as well know that neither riches nor opportunity would be available to us if ORGANIZED CAPITAL had not provided these benefits.

There is a principle known as the law of ECONOMICS! This is more than a theory. It is a law no one can beat. Remember the name of the principle because it is far more powerful than all the politicians and political machines. It is above and beyond the control of all the labor unions. It cannot be swayed, influenced, or bribed by racketeers or self-appointed leaders in any calling. Moreover, IT HAS AN ALL-SEEING EYE, AND A PERFECT SYSTEM OF BOOKKEEPING, in which it keeps an accurate account of the transactions of every human being engaged in the business of trying to get without giving. Sooner or later, its auditors come around, look over the records of individuals both great and small, and demand a reconciliation.

Wall Street, Big Business, Capital Predatory Interests, or whatever name you choose to give the system which has given us AMERICAN FREEDOM, represents a group of people who understand, respect, and adapt themselves to this powerful LAW OF ECONOMICS! Their financial continuation depends on respecting the law. Most people living in America like this country, its capitalistic system and all. I must confess I know of no better country where you can find greater opportunities to accumulate wealth. America provides all the freedom and all the opportunity to accumulate riches that any honest person may require. When one goes hunting for game, one selects hunting grounds where game is plentiful. When seeking riches, the same rule would naturally apply.

Behind all the exchange of merchandise and personal services, we seek out in this country, is an abundance of OPPORTUNITY to accumulate wealth. Here, AMERICAN FREEDOM comes to one's aid. There is nothing to stop you, or anyone from engaging in any portion of the effort necessary to carry on these businesses. If one has superior talent, training, and experience, one can accumulate riches in large amounts. Those not so fortunate can accumulate smaller amounts. Anyone can earn a living in return for a very nominal amount of labor.

So—there you are!

OPPORTUNITY has spread its wares before you. Step up to the front, select what you want, create your plan, put the plan into action, and follow through with PERSISTENCE. Capitalism will do the rest. You can depend on this much— CAPITALISM INSURES EVERY PERSON THE OPPORTUNITY TO CONTRIBUTE USEFUL SERVICE, AND TO COLLECT MONEY IN PROPORTION TO THE VALUE OF THE SERVICE. The "System" denies no one this right, but it does not, and cannot promise SOMETHING FOR NOTHING, because the system, itself, is irrevocably controlled by the LAW OF ECONOMICS which neither recognizes nor tolerates for long, GETTING WITHOUT GIVING. The LAW OF ECONOMICS was passed by nature! There is no Supreme Court to which violators of this law can appeal. The law hands out both penalties for its violation, and rewards for its observance, *without interference or the possibility of interference by any human being*. The law cannot be repealed. It is as fixed as the stars in the heavens, and subject to, and a part of the same system that controls the stars.

The practice, by government officials, of extending to men and women the privilege of raiding the public treasury in return for votes, sometimes results in election, but as night follows day, the final payoff comes; when every penny wrongfully used, must be repaid with compound interest on compound interest. If those who make the grab are not forced to repay, the burden falls on their children, and their children's children, "even unto the third and fourth generations." There is no way to avoid the debt. People can, and sometimes do, form groups to push wages up, and working hours down. There is a point beyond which they cannot go. It is the point at which the LAW OF ECONOMICS steps in, and the sheriff gets both the employer and the employees.

CHAPTER 7

DECISION

THE MASTERY OF PROCRASTINATION

ACCURATE ANALYSIS OF over 25,000 people who experienced failure, disclosed that LACK OF DECISION was near the head of the list of the 30 major causes of FAILURE. This is not just a theory—*it is a fact*. PROCRASTINATION, the opposite of DECISION, is a common enemy that almost everyone must conquer. You will have an opportunity to test your capacity to reach *quick* and *definite* DECISIONS when you finish reading this book, and are ready to begin putting into ACTION the principles it describes.

Analysis of several hundred people who had accumulated fortunes well beyond the million dollar mark, disclosed the fact that every one of them had the habit of REACHING DECISIONS PROMPTLY, and of changing these decisions SLOWLY, if and when they were changed. People who fail to accumulate money, *without exception*, have the habit of reaching decisions, IF AT ALL, very *slowly*, and of *changing these decisions quickly and often*. One of Henry Ford's most outstanding qualities was his *habit* of reaching decisions quickly and definitely, and changing them slowly. This quality was so pronounced in Mr. Ford, that it gave him the reputation of being obstinate. It was this quality which prompted Mr. Ford to continue to manufacture his famous Model "T" (the world's ugliest car), when his advisors, and many purchasers of the car, were urging him to change it. Perhaps, Mr. Ford delayed too long in making the change, but the other side of the story is, that Mr. Ford's firmness of decision yielded a huge fortune, before the change in model became *necessary*. There is little doubt that Mr. Ford's habit of definiteness of decision assumed the proportion of obstinacy, but this quality is preferable to slowness in reaching decisions and quickness in changing them.

The majority of people who fail to accumulate money sufficient for their needs, are, generally, easily influenced by the opinions of others. They permit the newspapers and the "gossiping" neighbors to do their thinking for them. Opinions are the cheapest commodities on earth. Everyone has a flock of opinions ready to be imposed anyone who will accept them. If you are influenced by opinions when you reach DECISIONS, you will not succeed in any undertaking, much less in that of transforming YOUR OWN DESIRE into money.

If you are influenced by the opinions of others, you will have no DESIRE of your own. Take your own advice, when you begin to put into practice the principles described here, by *reaching your own decisions* and following them. Take no one into your confidence, EXCEPT the members of your "Master Mind" group, and be very sure in your selection of this group, that you choose ONLY those who will be in COMPLETE SYMPATHY AND HARMONY WITH YOUR PURPOSE. Close friends and relatives, while not meaning to, often handicap us through opinions and sometimes through ridicule, which is meant to be humorous. Thousands of people carry inferiority complexes with them all through life, because some well-meaning, but ignorant person destroyed their confidence through opinions or ridicule.

You have a brain and mind of your own. USE IT and reach your own decisions. If you need facts or information from other people, to enable you to reach decisions, as you probably will in many instances; acquire these facts or secure the information you need quietly, without disclosing your purpose. It is characteristic of people who have only a smattering of knowledge to give the impression that they know much more. Such people generally do TOO MUCH talking, and TOO LITTLE listening. Keep your eyes and ears wide open—and your mouth CLOSED, if you wish to acquire the habit of prompt DECISION. Those who talk too much do little else. If you talk more than you listen, you not only deprive yourself of many opportunities to accumulate knowledge, but you also disclose your PLANS and PURPOSES to people who will take great delight in defeating you, because they envy you. Remember, also, that every time you open your mouth in the presence of a person who has an abundance of knowledge, you display to that person, your exact stock of knowledge, or your LACK of it! Genuine wisdom is usually conspicuous through *modesty and silence*.

Keep in mind the fact that every person you associate with is, like yourself, seeking the opportunity to accumulate money. If you talk about your plans too freely, you may be surprised when you learn that some other person has beaten you to your goal by PUTTING INTO ACTION AHEAD OF YOU, the plans of which you talked unwisely. Let one of your first decisions be to KEEP A CLOSED MOUTH AND OPEN EARS AND EYES. As a reminder to yourself to follow this advice, it will be helpful if you copy the following sentence in large letters and place it where you will see it daily.

"TELL THE WORLD WHAT YOU INTEND TO DO, BUT FIRST SHOW IT."

This is the equivalent of saying that "acts, and not words, are what count most."

FREEDOM OR DEATH ON A DECISION

The value of decisions depends on the courage required to make them. The great decisions, which served as the foundation of civilization, were reached by assuming great risks, which often meant the possibility of death. Lincoln's decision to issue his famous Emancipation Proclamation, which gave freedom to slaves, was rendered with full understanding that his act would turn thousands of friends and political supporters against him. He knew, too, that the carrying out of that proclamation would mean death to thousands of people on the battlefield. In the end, it cost Lincoln his life. That required courage.

Socrates' decision to drink the cup of poison, rather than compromise his personal belief, was a decision of courage. It turned time ahead a thousand years, and gave to future generations, the right to freedom of thought and speech. The decision of Gen. Robert E. Lee, when he came to the parting of the way with the Union, and took up the cause of the South, was a decision of courage, for he well knew that it might cost him his own life, that it would surely cost the lives of others. But, the greatest decision of all time, as far as any American citizen is concerned, was reached in Philadelphia, July 4, 1776, when fifty-six men signed their names to a document, which they well knew would bring freedom to all Americans, or *leave every one of the fifty-six hanging from a gallows!* You have heard of this famous document, but you may not have drawn from it the great lesson in personal achievement it so plainly taught.

We all remember the date of this momentous decision, but few of us realize what courage that decision required. We remember our history, as it was taught; we remember dates and the names of those who fought; we remember Valley Forge, and Yorktown; we remember George Washington, and Lord Cornwallis. But we know little of the real forces behind these names, dates, and places. We know even less of that intangible POWER, which insured us freedom *long before Washington's armies reached Yorktown.* We read the history of the Revolution, and falsely imagine that George Washington was the Father of our Country, that it was he who won our freedom, while the truth is Washington was only an accessory after the fact, because victory for his armies had been insured long before Lord Cornwallis surrendered. This is not intended to rob Washington of any of the glory he so richly earned. Its purpose, rather, is to give greater attention to the astounding POWER that was the real cause of his victory.

It is nothing short of tragedy that the writers of history have missed, entirely, even the slightest reference to the irresistible POWER, which gave birth and freedom to the nation destined to set up new standards of independence for all people of the earth. I say it is a tragedy, because it is the same POWER that must be used by everyone who surmounts the difficulties of Life and forces Life to pay the price. Let us briefly review the events that gave birth to this POWER. The story begins with an incident in Boston, March 5, 1770. British soldiers were patrolling the streets, openly threatening the citizens. The colonists resented armed men marching in their midst. They began to express their resentment openly, hurling stones as well as epithets, at the marching soldiers, until the commanding officer gave orders, "Fix bayonets. . . . Charge!"

The battle was on. It resulted in the death and injury of many. The incident aroused such resentment that the Provincial Assembly, (made up of prominent colonists), called a meeting for taking definite action. Two of the members of that Assembly were John Hancock and Samuel Adams—LONG LIVE THEIR NAMES! They spoke up courageously and declared that a move must be made to eject all British soldiers from Boston. Remember this—a DECISION, in the minds of two men, might properly be called the beginning of the freedom which we now enjoy. Remember, too, that the DECISION of these two men called for FAITH and COURAGE, because it was dangerous. Before the Assembly adjourned, Samuel Adams was appointed to call on the Governor of the Province, Hutchinson, and demand the withdrawal of the British troops.

The request was granted, the troops were removed from Boston, but the incident was not closed. It had caused a situation destined to change the entire trend of civilization. Strange, is it not, how the great changes, such as the American Revolution and the World War, often have their beginnings in circumstances that seem unimportant? It is interesting, also that these important changes usually begin in the form of a DEFINITE DECISION in the minds of a relatively small number of people. Few of us know the history of our country well enough to realize that John Hancock, Samuel Adams, and Richard Henry Lee (of the Province of Virginia) were the real Fathers of our Country.

Richard Henry Lee became an important factor in this story because he and Samuel Adams communicated frequently (by correspondence), sharing freely their fears and their hopes concerning the welfare of the people of their Provinces. From this practice, Adams conceived the idea that a mutual exchange of letters between the thirteen Colonies might help to bring about the coordination of effort so badly needed in connection with the solution of their problems. Two years after the clash with the soldiers in Boston (March '72), Adams presented this idea to the Assembly, in the form of a motion that a Correspondence Committee be established among the Colonies, with definitely appointed correspondents in each Colony, "for the purpose of friendly cooperation for the betterment of the Colonies of British America."

Remember this incident! It was the beginning of the organization of the far-flung POWER destined to give freedom to you and to me. The Master Mind had already been organized. It consisted of Adams, Lee, and Hancock. The Committee of Correspondence was organized. This move provided the way for increasing the power of the Master Mind by adding to it men from all the Colonies. This was the first ORGANIZED PLANNING of the disgruntled Colonists. In union there is strength! The citizens of the Colonies had been waging disorganized warfare against the British soldiers, through incidents similar to the Boston riot, but nothing of benefit had been accomplished. Their individual grievances had not been consolidated under one Master Mind. No group of individuals had put their hearts, minds, souls, and bodies together in one definite DECISION to settle their difficulty with the British once and for all, until Adams, Hancock, and Lee got together.

Meanwhile, the British were not idle. They, too, were doing some PLANNING and "Master-Minding" of their own, with the advantage of money and organized soldiery. The Crown appointed Gage to replace Hutchinson as the Governor of

Massachusetts. One of the new Governor's first acts was to send a messenger to call on Samuel Adams, to stop his opposition—through FEAR. We can best understand the spirit of what happened by quoting the conversation between Col. Fenton, (the messenger sent by Gage), and Adams.

Col. Fenton: "I have been authorized by Governor Gage, to assure you, Mr. Adams, that the Governor has been empowered to confer upon you such benefits as would be satisfactory, [endeavor to win Adams by promise of bribes], on the condition that you cease opposition to the measures of the government. It is the Governor's advice to you, Sir, not to incur the further displeasure of his majesty. Your conduct makes you liable to penalties of an Act of Henry VIII, by which persons can be sent to England for trial for treason, or misprision of treason, at the discretion of a governor of a province. But, BY CHANGING YOUR POLITICAL COURSE, you will not only gain great personal advantages, but you will make peace with the King."

Samuel Adams had the choice of two DECISIONS. He could cease his opposition, and receive personal bribes, or he could CONTINUE, AND RUN THE RISK OF BEING HANGED! Clearly, the time had come when Adams was *forced* to reach *instantly*, a DECISION which could have cost his life. Most people would have found it difficult to reach such a decision. The majority would have sent back an evasive reply, but not Adams! He insisted on Col. Fenton's word of honor, that the Colonel would deliver to the Governor the answer exactly as Adams would give it to him.

Adams' answer: "Then you may tell Governor Gage that I trust I have long since made my peace with the King of Kings. No personal consideration can convince me to abandon the cause of my Country. And, TELL GOVERNOR GAGE IT IS THE ADVICE OF SAMUEL ADAMS TO HIM, no longer to insult the feelings of an exasperated people."

Comment as to the character of this man seems unnecessary. It must be obvious to all who read this astounding message that its sender possessed loyalty of the highest order. *This is important.* (Racketeers and dishonest politicians have prostituted the honor for which such men as Adams died).

When Governor Gage received Adams' caustic reply, he flew into a rage, and issued a proclamation which read, "I do, hereby, in his majesty's name, offer and promise his most gracious pardon to all persons who shall forthwith lay down their arms, and return to the duties of peaceable subjects, excepting only from the benefit of such pardon, SAMUEL ADAMS AND JOHN HANCOCK, whose offences are of too flagitious a nature to admit of any other consideration but that of condign punishment."

As one might say, in modern slang, Adams and Hancock were "on the spot!" The threat of the irate Governor forced the two men to reach another DECISION, equally as dangerous. They hurriedly called a secret meeting of their staunchest followers. (Here the Master Mind began to take on momentum). After the meeting had been called to order, Adams locked the door, placed the key in his pocket, and informed all present that it was imperative that a Congress of the Colonists be organized, and that

NO ONE WOULD LEAVE THE ROOM UNTIL THE DECISION FOR SUCH A CONGRESS HAD BEEN REACHED.

Great excitement followed. Some weighed the possible consequences of such radicalism. Some expressed grave doubt as to the wisdom of so *definite a decision* in defiance of the Crown. Locked in that room were TWO MEN immune to Fear, blind to the possibility of Failure. Hancock and Adams. Through their influence, the others agreed that, through the Correspondence Committee, arrangements should be made for a meeting of the First Continental Congress, to be held in Philadelphia, September 5, 1774. Remember this date. It is more important than July 4, 1776. If there had been no DECISION to hold a Continental Congress, there could have been no signing of the Declaration of Independence.

Before the first meeting of the new Congress, another leader, in a different section of the country was deep in the throes of publishing a "Summary View of the Rights of British America." He was Thomas Jefferson, of the Province of Virginia, whose relationship to Lord Dunmore (representative of the Crown in Virginia) was as strained as that of Hancock and Adams with their Governor. Shortly after his famous Summary of Rights was published, Jefferson was informed that he was subject to prosecution for high treason against his majesty's government. Inspired by the threat, one of Jefferson's colleagues, Patrick Henry, boldly spoke his mind, concluding his remarks with: "*If this be treason, then make the most of it.*"

It was such men as these who, without power, without authority, without military strength, without money, sat in solemn consideration of the destiny of the colonies, beginning at the opening of the First Continental Congress, and continuing at intervals for two years—until on June 7, 1776, Richard Henry Lee arose, addressed the Chair, and to the startled Assembly made this motion:

"Gentlemen, I make the motion that these United Colonies are, and of right ought to be free and independent states, that they be absolved from all allegiance to the British Crown, and that all political connection between them and the state of Great Britain is, and ought to be totally dissolved."

Lee's astounding motion was discussed fervently, and at such length that he began to lose patience. Finally, after days of argument, he again took the floor and declared in a clear, firm voice, "Mr. President, we have discussed this issue for days. It is the only course for us to follow. Why, then Sir, do we longer delay? Why still deliberate? Let this happy day give birth to an American Republic. Let her arise, not to devastate and to conquer, but to reestablish peace and law. The eyes of Europe are fixed upon us. She demands of us a living example of freedom that may exhibit a contrast, in the felicity of the citizen, to the ever increasing tyranny."

Before his motion was finally voted on, Lee was called back to Virginia, because of a serious family illness, but before leaving, he placed his cause in the hands of his friend, Thomas Jefferson, who promised to fight until favorable action was taken. Soon after, the President of the Congress (Hancock), appointed Jefferson as Chairman of a Committee to draw up a Declaration of Independence. Long and hard the Committee labored, on a document which would mean, when accepted by the

Congress, that EVERY ONE WHO SIGNED IT, WOULD BE SIGNING HIS OWN DEATH WARRANT, should the Colonies lose in the fight with Great Britain, which was sure to follow. The document was drawn, and on June 28, the original draft was read before the Congress. For several days it was discussed, altered, and made ready. On July 4, 1776, Thomas Jefferson stood before the Assembly, and fearlessly read the most momentous DECISION ever placed on paper.

"When in the course of human events it is necessary for one people to dissolve the political bands which have connected them with another, and to assume, among the powers of the earth, the separate and equal station to which the laws of Nature, and of Nature's God entitle them, a decent respect to the opinions of mankind requires that they should declare the causes which impel them to the separation. . . ."

When Jefferson finished, the document was voted on, accepted, and signed by the fifty-six men, every one staking his own life on the DECISION to write his name. By that DECISION came into existence a nation destined to bring to mankind forever, the privilege of making DECISIONS. By decisions made in a similar spirit of Faith, and only by such decisions, can we solve our personal problems, and win for ourselves high estates of material and spiritual wealth. Let us not forget this! Analyze the events that led to the Declaration of Independence, and be convinced that this nation, which now holds a position of commanding respect and power among all nations of the world, was born of a DECISION created by a Master Mind, consisting of fifty-six men. Note well, the fact that it was their DECISION that insured the success of Washington's armies, because the spirit of that decision was in the heart of every soldier who fought with him, and served as a spiritual power which recognizes no such thing as FAILURE.

Note, also, (with great personal benefit), that the POWER that gave this nation its freedom, is the same power that must be used by every individual who becomes self-determining. This POWER is made up of the principles described in this book. It will not be difficult to detect, in the story of the Declaration of Independence, at least six of these principles; DESIRE, DECISION, FAITH, PERSISTENCE, THE MASTER MIND, and ORGANIZED PLANNING. Throughout this philosophy will be found the suggestion that thought, backed by strong DESIRE, has a tendency to transform itself into its physical equivalent. Before passing on, I wish to leave with you the suggestion that one may find in this story, and in the story of the organization of the United States Steel Corporation, a perfect description of the method by which thought makes this astounding transformation.

In your search for the secret of the method, do not look for a miracle, because you will not find it. You will find only the eternal laws of Nature. These laws are available to every person who has the FAITH and the COURAGE to use them. They may be used to bring freedom to a nation or to accumulate wealth. There is no cost other than the time necessary to understand and implement them. Those who reach DECISIONS promptly and definitely, know what they want, and generally get it. The leaders in every walk of life DECIDE quickly and firmly. That is the major reason why they are leaders. The world has the habit of making room for people whose words and actions show that they know where they're going.

INDECISION is a habit that usually begins in youth. The habit takes on permanency as the youth goes through grade school, high school, and even through college, without DEFINITENESS OF PURPOSE. The major weakness of all educational systems is that they neither teach nor encourage the habit of DEFINITE DECISION. It would be beneficial if no college would permit the enrollment of any student, unless and until the student declared a major. It would be of still greater benefit, if every student entering grade school was trained in the HABIT OF DECISION, and required to pass an exam on this subject before advancing to the next grade level. The habit of INDECISION acquired because of the deficiencies of our school systems, goes with students into the occupations they choose . . . IF . . . in fact, they choose an occupation. Generally, the youth just out of school seek any job that can be found. They take the first one they find, because they are in the habit of INDECISION. Ninety-eight out of every hundred people, working for wages today, are in the positions they hold because they lacked the DEFINITENESS OF DECISION to PLAN A DEFINITE POSITION, and the knowledge of how to choose an employer.

DEFINITENESS OF DECISION always requires courage, sometimes very great courage. The fifty-six men who signed the Declaration of Independence staked their lives on the DECISION to affix their signatures to that document. People who reach a DEFINITE DECISION to get a particular job, and make life pay the price it asks, do not stake life on that decision; they stake their ECONOMIC FREEDOM. Financial independence, wealth, desirable business and professional positions are not within reach of the person who neglects or refuses to EXPECT, PLAN, and DEMAND these things. The person who desires riches in the same spirit that Samuel Adams desired freedom for the Colonies, is sure to accumulate wealth.

CHAPTER 8

PERSISTENCE

THE SUSTAINED EFFORT NECESSARY TO INDUCE FAITH

PERSISTENCE IS ESSENTIAL for transforming DESIRE into its monetary equivalent. The basis of persistence is the POWER OF WILL. Will-power and desire, when properly combined, make an irresistible pair. People who accumulate great fortunes are generally considered lucky and sometimes called ruthless. Often they are misunderstood. What they have is will-power, which they mix with persistence, and place behind their desires to insure the attainment of their goals. Henry Ford has been generally misunderstood to be ruthless and cold-blooded. This misconception grew out of Ford's habit of following through in all of his plans with PERSISTENCE.

The majority of people are ready to throw their aims and purposes overboard, and give up at the first sign of opposition or misfortune. A few carry on DESPITE all opposition, until they reach their goal. These few are the Fords, Carnegies, Rockefellers, and Edisons. There may be no heroic connotation to the word "persistence," but persistence is to character what carbon is to steel. The building of a fortune, generally, involves the application of the entire thirteen factors of this philosophy. These principles must be understood, they must be applied with PERSISTENCE by all who want to accumulate money.

If you are following this book with the intention of applying the knowledge it conveys, your first of PERSISTENCE will come when you begin to follow the six steps described in the second chapter. Unless you are one of the two out of every hundred who already have a DEFINITE GOAL at which you are aiming, and a DEFINITE PLAN for its attainment, you may read the instructions, and then pass on with your daily routine, and never comply with those instructions. Lack of persistence is one of the major causes of failure. Moreover, experience with thousands of people has proven that lack of persistence is a weakness common in most people. It is a weakness that can be overcome by effort. The ease with which lack of persistence may be conquered will depend *entirely* upon the INTENSITY OF

YOUR DESIRE. The starting point of all achievement is DESIRE. Keep this constantly in mind. Weak desires bring weak results, just as a small amount of fire makes a small amount of heat. If you find yourself lacking persistence, this weakness can be remedied by building a stronger fire under your desires. Continue to read through to the end, then go back to Chapter two, and start *immediately* to carry out the instructions given in connection with the six steps. The eagerness with which you follow these instructions will indicate clearly, how much, or how little you really DESIRE money. If you are indifferent, you have not yet acquired the "money consciousness" that you must possess before you can be sure of accumulating a fortune.

Fortunes gravitate to people whose minds have been prepared to "attract" them, just as surely as water moves downhill. This book contains all the stimuli necessary to "attune" any normal mind to the vibrations that will attract the object of one's desires. If you find you are weak in PERSISTENCE, center your attention on the instructions contained in the chapter on "Power"; surround yourself with a "MASTER MIND" group, and through the cooperative efforts of the members of this group, you can develop persistence. You will find additional instructions for the development of persistence in the chapters on auto-suggestion, and the subconscious mind. Follow the instructions outlined in these chapters until your habit nature hands over to your subconscious mind, a clear picture of what you DESIRE. From that point on, you will not be handicapped by lack of persistence.

Your subconscious mind works continuously while you are awake and while you are asleep. Spasmodic or occasional effort to apply the rules will be of no value. To get RESULTS, you must apply all of the rules until their application becomes a fixed habit. In no other way can you develop the necessary "money consciousness." POVERTY is attracted to the one whose mind is favorable to it, as money is attracted to the one whose mind has been deliberately prepared to attract it, and through the same laws. POVERTY CONSCIOUSNESS WILL VOLUNTARILY SEIZE THE MIND THAT IS NOT OCCUPIED WITH THE MONEY CONSCIOUSNESS.

Catch the full significance of the statements in the previous paragraph, and you will understand the importance of PERSISTENCE in the accumulation of a fortune. Without PERSISTENCE, you will be defeated, even before you start. With PERSISTENCE you will win. If you have ever experienced a nightmare, you realize the value of persistence. You are lying in bed, half awake, with a feeling that you are about to die. You are unable to turn over or to move a muscle. You realize that you MUST BEGIN to regain control over your muscles. Through persistent effort of will-power, you finally manage to move the fingers of one hand. By continuing to move your fingers, you extend your control to the muscles of one arm, until you can lift it. Then you gain control of the other arm in the same manner. You finally gain control over the muscles of one leg, and then extend it to the other leg. THEN—WITH ONE SUPREME EFFORT OF WILL—you regain complete control over your muscular system, and "snap" out of your nightmare. The trick has been turned step by step.

You may find it necessary to "snap" out of your mental inertia, through a similar procedure, moving slowly at first, then increasing your speed, until you gain complete control over your will. Be PERSISTENT no matter how slowly you may, at first, have to move. WITH PERSISTENCE WILL COME SUCCESS. If you select your "Master Mind" group with care, you will have in it, at least one person who will aid you in the development of PERSISTENCE. Some who have accumulated great fortunes, did so because of NECESSITY. They developed the habit of PERSISTENCE, because they were so closely driven by circumstances, that they *had to become persistent.* THERE IS NO SUBSTITUTE FOR PERSISTENCE! It cannot be substituted with any other quality! Remember this and it will hearten you in the beginning, when the going seems difficult and slow.

Those who have cultivated the HABIT of persistence seem to enjoy insurance against failure. No matter how many times they are defeated, they finally arrive up toward the top of the ladder. Sometimes it appears that there is a hidden Guide whose duty is to test us through all sorts of discouraging experiences. Those who pick themselves up after defeat and keep on trying, arrive; and the world cries, "Bravo! I knew you could do it!" The hidden Guide lets no one enjoy great achievement without passing the PERSISTENCE TEST. Those who can't take it, simply do not make the grade. Those who can "take it" are bountifully rewarded for their PERSISTENCE. They receive, as their compensation, whatever goal they are pursuing. That is not all! They receive something infinitely more important than material compensation—the knowledge that "EVERY FAILURE BRINGS WITH IT THE SEED OF AN EQUIVALENT ADVANTAGE."

There are exceptions to this rule; a few people know from experience the soundness of persistence. They are the ones who have not accepted defeat as being anything more than temporary. They are the ones whose DESIRES are so PERSISTENTLY APPLIED that defeat is finally changed into victory. We who stand on the side-lines of Life see the overwhelmingly large number who go down in defeat, never to rise again. We see the few who take the punishment of defeat *as an urge to greater effort.* These, fortunately, never learn to accept Life's reverse gear. But what we DO NOT SEE, what most of us never suspect of existing, is the silent but irresistible POWER which comes to the rescue of those who fight on in the face of discouragement. If we speak of this power at all, we call it PERSISTENCE and let it go at that. One thing we all know, without PERSISTENCE, one cannot achieve noteworthy success in any calling.

As these lines are being written, I look up from my work, and see before me, less than a block away, the great mysterious "Broadway," the "Graveyard of Dead Hopes," and the "Front Porch of Opportunity." From all over the world, people have come to Broadway, seeking fame, fortune, power, love, or whatever it is that human beings call success. Once in a great while someone steps out from the long procession of seekers, and the world hears that another person has mastered Broadway. But Broadway is not conquered quickly or easily. It acknowledges talent, recognizes genius, pays off in money, only *after* one has refused to QUIT. That's when we know someone has discovered the secret to Broadway. The secret is always inseparably attached to one word, PERSISTENCE!

The secret is told in the struggle of Fannie Hurst, whose PERSISTENCE conquered the Great White Way. She came to New York in 1915, to convert writing into riches. The conversion did not come quickly, BUT IT CAME. For four years, Miss Hurst learned about "The Sidewalks of New York" from firsthand experience. She spent her days laboring and her nights HOPING. When hope grew dim, she did not say, "Alright Broadway, you win!" She said, "Very well, Broadway, you may whip some, but not me. I'm going to force you to give up."

One publisher (The Saturday Evening Post) sent her *thirty six* rejection slips, before she "broke the ice" and got a story across. The average writer, like the "average" in other walks of life, would have given up the job when the first rejection slip came. She pounded the pavements for four years to the tune of the publisher's "NO," because she was determined to win. Then came the "payoff." The spell had been broken, the unseen Guide had tested Fannie Hurst, and she could take it. From that time on, publishers made a beaten path to her door. Money came so fast she hardly had time to count it. Then the movie industry discovered her, and money came not in small change, but in floods. The motion picture rights to her novel, "Great Laughter," brought $100,000.00, said to be the highest price ever paid at that time in history.

Before leaving the subject of PERSISTENCE, take inventory of yourself, and determine in what particular, if any, you are lacking in this essential quality. Measure yourself courageously, point by point, and see how many of the eight factors of persistence you lack. The analysis may lead to discoveries that will give you a new grip on yourself.

SYMPTOMS OF LACK OF PERSISTENCE

Here you will find the real enemies that stand between you and noteworthy achievement. Here you will find not only the "symptoms" indicating weakness of PERSISTENCE, but also the deeply seated subconscious causes of this weakness. Study the list carefully, and face yourself squarely IF YOU REALLY WISH TO KNOW WHO YOU ARE AND WHAT YOU ARE CAPABLE OF DOING. The following weaknesses must be mastered before you can accumulate wealth:

- Failure to recognize and to clearly define exactly what you want.
- Procrastination, with or without cause. (Usually backed up with a formidable array of excuses).
- Lack of interest in acquiring specialized knowledge.
- Indecision, the habit of "passing the buck" on all occasions, instead of facing issues squarely. (Also backed with excuses).
- The habit of relying on excuses instead of creating definite plans for the solution of problems.

PRINCIPLES OF PERSISTENCE

Persistence is a state of mind, therefore it can be cultivated. Like all states of mind, persistence is based on definite causes. The key principles of persistence are listed below. Rank yourself 0-5, 0 having no possession of the principle, 5 having mastery over it.

DEFINITENESS OF PURPOSE. Knowing what you want is the first and, perhaps, the most important step toward the development of persistence. A strong motive helps us surmount many difficulties.

DESIRE. It is comparatively easy to acquire and to maintain persistence in pursuing the object of intense desire

SELF-RELIANCE. Belief in your ability to carry out a plan encourages you to follow the plan through with persistence.

DEFINITENESS OF PLANS. Organized plans, even though they may be weak and entirely impractical, encourage persistence.

ACCURATE KNOWLEDGE. Knowing that your plans are sound, based upon experience or observation, encourages persistence; "guessing" instead of "knowing" destroys persistence.

CO-OPERATION. Sympathy, understanding, and harmonious cooperation with others tend to develop persistence.

WILL-POWER. The habit of concentrating you thoughts on the building of plans for the attainment of a definite purpose, leads to persistence.

HABIT. Persistence is the direct result of habit. The mind absorbs and becomes a part of the daily experiences upon which it feeds. Fear, the worst of all enemies, can be effectively cured by *forced acts of courage*. Anyone who has seen active service in war knows this.

- Indifference, usually reflected by the willingness to compromise on all occasions, rather than meet opposition and fight it.
- The habit of blaming others for your mistakes, and accepting bad circumstances as being unavoidable.
- WEAKNESS OF DESIRE, due to neglect in the choice of MOTIVES that impel action.
- Willingness, even eagerness, to quit at the first sign of defeat. (Based on one or more of the 6 basic fears).
- Lack of ORGANIZED PLANS, placed in writing where they may be analyzed.
- The habit of neglecting to move on ideas, or to grasp opportunity when it presents itself.
- WISHING instead of WILLING.
- The habit of compromising with MEDIOCRITY instead of aiming at wealth.
- General absence of ambition to *be*, to *do*, and to *own*.
- Searching for all the short-cuts to riches, trying to GET without GIVING a fair equivalent, usually reflected in the habit of gambling, endeavoring to drive "sharp" bargains.
- FEAR OF CRITICISM, failure to create plans and to put them into action, because of what other people will think, do, or say. This enemy belongs at the head of the list, because it generally exists in the subconscious mind, where its presence is not recognized.

Let us examine some of the symptoms of the Fear of Criticism. Most people permit relatives, friends, and the public at large to influence them to the extent that they cannot live their own lives, because they fear criticism. Huge numbers of people make mistakes in marriage, stand by the bargain, and go through life miserable and unhappy, because they fear the criticism that will follow if they correct the mistake. (Anyone who has submitted to this form of fear knows the irreparable damage it does, by destroying ambition, self-reliance, and the desire to achieve).

Millions of people neglect to go back to school, after having left, because they fear criticism. Countless people, both young and old, permit relatives to wreck their lives in the name of DUTY, because they fear criticism. (Duty does not require us to submit to the destruction of our personal ambitions and the right to live our lives as we wish). People refuse to take chances in business because they fear the criticism if they fail. *The fear of criticism, in such cases, is stronger than the DESIRE for success.*

Too many people refuse to set high goals for themselves, or even neglect selecting a career, because they fear the criticism of relatives and "friends."

When Andrew Carnegie suggested that I devote twenty years to the organization of a philosophy of individual achievement, my first impulse of thought was fear of what people might say. The suggestion set up a goal for me, far larger than any goal I'd ever pursued. As quick as a flash, my mind began to create excuses, all of them traceable to the inherent FEAR OF CRITICISM. Something inside of me said, "You can't do it—the job is too big and requires too much time. What will *other* people think about this idea? How will you earn a living? No one has ever organized a philosophy of success, what right have you to believe you can do it? Who are you, anyway? Remember your humble beginnings—what do you know about philosophy— people will think you are crazy (and they did). If it's such a good idea, why hasn't someone done it before?"

These, and many other questions flashed into my mind, and demanded attention. It seemed as if the whole world had suddenly turned its attention to me with the purpose of ridiculing me into giving up all desire to carry out Mr. Carnegie's suggestion. I had a fine opportunity, then and there, to kill off ambition before it gained control of me. Later in life, after having analyzed thousands of people, I discovered that MOST IDEAS ARE STILLBORN, AND NEED THE BREATH OF LIFE INJECTED INTO THEM THROUGH DEFINITE PLANS OF IMMEDIATE ACTION. The time to nurse an idea is at the time of its birth. Every minute it lives, gives it a better chance of surviving. The FEAR OF CRITICISM is the cause of destruction of most ideas that never reach the PLANNING and ACTION stage.

LUCKY BREAKS

Many people believe that material success is the result of favorable "breaks." There is an element of truth in the belief, but those depending entirely on luck are nearly always disappointed, because they overlook another important factor that must be present to ensure success. It is the knowledge with which favorable "breaks" can be made to order. During the great depression, W. C. Fields, the comedian, lost all his money, and found himself without income, without a job, and his means of earning a living (vaudeville) no longer existed. Moreover, he was past sixty, when many people consider themselves "old." He was so eager to stage a comeback that he offered to work without pay, in a new field (movies). In addition to his other troubles, he fell and injured his neck. To many, that would have been the place to give up and QUIT. But Fields was PERSISTENT. He knew that if he carried on he would get the "break" sooner or later, and he did, but not by chance.

Marie Dressler found herself down and out, with her money gone, with no job, when she was about sixty. She, too, went after the "breaks," and got them. Her PERSISTENCE brought an astounding triumph late in life, long beyond the age when most people are done with ambition to achieve. Eddie Cantor lost his money in the 1929 stock crash, but he still had his PERSISTENCE and his courage. With these, plus two prominent eyes, he exploited himself back into an income of $10,000 a week! If one has PERSISTENCE, one can get along very well without many other qualities.

The only "break" anyone can afford to rely on is a self-made "break." These come through the application of PERSISTENCE. The starting point is DEFINITENESS OF PURPOSE. Examine the first hundred people you meet, ask them what they want most in life, and ninety eight of them will not be able to tell you. If you press them for an answer, some will say SECURITY, many will say MONEY, a few will say

DEVELOPING PERSISTENCE

There are four simple steps that lead to the habit of PERSISTENCE. They call for no great amount of intelligence, no particular amount of education, and little time or effort. The necessary steps are:

1. A DEFINITE PURPOSE BACKED BY BURNING DESIRE FOR ITS FULFILLMENT. What is your definite purpose?

   _____

2. A DEFINITE PLAN, EXPRESSED IN CONTINUOUS ACTION. Do you have a definite plan? Where is it outlined?

   _____

3. A MIND CLOSED TIGHTLY AGAINST ALL NEGATIVE AND DISCOURAGING INFLUENCES, including negative suggestions from relatives, friends, and acquaintances. What remaining negative influences do you need to avoid or learn to shield yourself against?

   _____

4. A FRIENDLY ALLIANCE WITH ONE OR MORE PERSONS WHO WILL ENCOURAGE YOU TO FOLLOW THROUGH WITH BOTH PLAN AND PURPOSE. Who are your alliances?

   _____

HAPPINESS. Others will say FAME AND POWER, and still others will say SOCIAL RECOGNITION, EASE IN LIVING, ABILITY TO SING, DANCE, or WRITE, but none of them will be able to define these terms, or give the slightest indication of a PLAN by which they hope to attain these vaguely expressed wishes. Wealth does not respond to wishes. It responds only to definite plans, backed by definite desires, through constant PERSISTENCE.

The box on the previous pages describes four steps that are essential for success in all walks of life. The entire purpose of the thirteen principles of this philosophy is to enable you to make these four steps *habit*.

These are the steps by which you can control your economic destiny.

They are the steps that lead to freedom and independence of thought.

They are the steps that lead to money, in small or great quantities.

They lead the way to power, fame, and worldly recognition.

They are the four steps that guarantee favorable "breaks."

They are the steps that convert dreams into physical realities.

They lead, also, to the mastery of FEAR, DISCOURAGEMENT, and INDIFFERENCE.

There is a magnificent reward for all who learn to use these four steps. It is the privilege of writing your own ticket, and of making Life yield whatever is asked. Take King Edward, for example, what lesson can we learn from his part in the world's greatest drama of historic times? Did he pay too high a price for the affections of the woman of his choice? Surely no one but he can give the correct answer. The rest of us can only guess. This much we know, the king came into the world without his own consent. He was born to great riches, without requesting them. He was persistently sought in marriage; politicians and statesmen throughout Europe tossed matriarchs and princesses at his feet. Because he was the first born of his parents, he inherited a crown, which he did not seek, and perhaps did not desire. For more than forty years, he was not a free agent, could not live his life in his own way, had little privacy, and finally assumed duties inflicted on him when he ascended the throne.

Some will say, "With all these blessings, King Edward should have found peace of mind, contentment, and joy of living." The truth is, behind all the privileges of a crown, all the money, the fame, and the power inherited by King Edward, there was an emptiness which could be filled only by love. His greatest DESIRE was for love. Long before he met Wallis Simpson, he doubtless felt this great universal emotion tugging at the strings of his heart, beating on the door of his soul, and crying out for expression. And when he met a kindred spirit, crying out for this same Holy privilege of expression, he recognized it, and without fear or apology, opened his heart and allowed it to enter. All the scandal-mongers in the world cannot destroy the beauty of this international drama, through which two people found love, and had the courage to face open criticism, renounce ALL ELSE to give it *holy* expression.

King Edward's DECISION to give up the crown of the world's most powerful empire, for the privilege of going the remainder of the way through life with the woman of his choice, was a decision that required courage. The decision also had a price, but who has the right to say the price was too great? Surely not He who said, "He among you who is without sin, let him cast the first stone." As a suggestion to any evil-minded person who chooses to find fault with the Duke of Windsor, because his DESIRE was for LOVE, and for openly declaring his love for Wallis Simpson, and giving up his throne for her, let it be remembered that the OPEN DECLARATION was not essential. He could have followed the custom of secret affairs that has prevailed in Europe for centuries, without giving up either his throne or the woman of his choice, and there would have been NO COMPLAINT FROM EITHER CHURCH OR LAITY. But this unusual man was built of sterner stuff. His love was clean. It was deep and sincere. It represented the one thing that, above ALL ELSE he truly DESIRED. He took what he wanted, and paid the price demanded.

In the words of Stuart Austin Wier we raise our cup and drink this toast to ex-king Edward and Wallis Simpson:

"Blessed is the man who has come to know that our muted thoughts are our sweetest thoughts.

"Blessed is the man who, from the blackest depths, can see the luminous figure of LOVE, and seeing, sing; and singing, say: 'Sweeter far than uttered lays are the thoughts I have of you.'"

In these words, we pay tribute to the two people who, more than all others of modern times, have been the victims of criticism and the recipients of abuse, because they found Life's greatest treasure, and claimed it. Most of the world applauds the Duke of Windsor and Wallis Simpson, because of their PERSISTENCE in searching until they found life's greatest reward. ALL OF US CAN PROFIT by following their example in our own search for that which we demand of life. What mystical power gives people of PERSISTENCE the capacity to master difficulties? Does the quality of PERSISTENCE set up in one's mind some form of spiritual, mental, or chemical activity which gives one access to supernatural forces? Does Infinite Intelligence throw itself on the side of the person who still fights on, after the battle has been lost, with the whole world on the opposing side?

These and many other similar questions have arisen in my mind as I have observed people like Henry Ford, who started from scratch and built an Industrial Empire of huge proportions, with little else in the way of a beginning but PERSISTENCE. Or, Thomas Edison, who, with less than three months of schooling, became the world's leading inventor and converted PERSISTENCE into the record player, the motion picture, and the light bulb, to say nothing of half a hundred other useful inventions.

As one makes an impartial study of the prophets, philosophers, "miracle" men, and religious leaders of the past, one is drawn to the inevitable conclusion that PERSISTENCE, concentration of effort, and DEFINITENESS OF PURPOSE, were the major sources of their achievements. Consider, for example, the strange and fascinating story of Mohammed; analyze his life, compare him with people of achievement in this modern age of technology, and observe how they have one outstanding trait in common, PERSISTENCE!

CHAPTER 9

THE MASTER MIND

THE DRIVING FORCE

POWER IS ESSENTIAL for success in the accumulation of money. PLANS are inert and useless without sufficient POWER to translate them into ACTION. This chapter will describe the method by which an individual may attain and apply POWER. POWER may be defined as "organized and intelligently directed KNOWLEDGE." Here, power refers to ORGANIZED effort, sufficient to enable an individual to transform DESIRE into its monetary equivalent. ORGANIZED effort is produced through the coordination of effort of two or more people, who work toward a DEFINITE end, in a spirit of harmony.

POWER IS REQUIRED FOR THE ACCUMULATION OF MONEY! POWER IS NECESSARY FOR THE RETENTION OF MONEY AFTER IT HAS BEEN ACCUMULATED! How is power acquired? If power is "organized knowledge," let us examine the sources of knowledge:

- INFINITE INTELLIGENCE. This source of knowledge may be contacted through the procedure previously described, with the aid of Creative Imagination.

- ACCUMULATED EXPERIENCE. The accumulated experience of a person, (or that portion of it which has been organized and recorded), may be found in any well-equipped public library. An important part of this accumulated experience is taught in public schools and colleges, where it has been classified and organized.

- EXPERIMENT AND RESEARCH. In the field of science, and in practically every other walk of life, people are gathering, classifying, and organizing new facts daily. This is the source to which one must turn when knowledge is not available through "accumulated experience." Here, too, the Creative Imagination must often be used.

Knowledge may be acquired from any of those sources. It may be converted into POWER by organizing it into definite PLANS and by expressing those plans in terms of ACTION. Examination of the three major sources of knowledge quickly reveals the difficulty people would have, if they relies solely on their own efforts, in assembling knowledge and expressing it through definite plans in terms of ACTION. If your plans are comprehensive, and if they contemplate large proportions, you must convince others to cooperate with you before you can inject into them the necessary element of POWER.

GAINING POWER THROUGH THE "MASTER MIND"

The "Master Mind" may be defined as: Coordination of knowledge and effort, in a spirit of harmony, between two or more people, for the attainment of a definite purpose.

No individual may have great power without the "Master Mind." In a preceding chapter, instructions were given for the creation of PLANS for translating DESIRE into its monetary equivalent. If you carry out these instructions with PERSISTENCE and intelligence, and use discrimination in the selection of your "Master Mind" group, your objective will have been half-way reached, even before you begin to recognize it.

To understand the "intangible" potential of power available to you, through a properly chosen "Master Mind" group, we will explain the two characteristics of the Master Mind principle, one of which is economic in nature, and the other psychic. The economic feature is obvious. Economic advantages may be created by anyone who surrounds themselves with the advice, counsel, and personal cooperation of a group of people who are willing to lend wholehearted aid, in a spirit of PERFECT HARMONY. This form of cooperative alliance has been the basis of nearly every great fortune. Your understanding of this great truth will definitely determine your financial status.

The psychic phase of the Master Mind principle is much more abstract, much more difficult to comprehend, because it has reference to the spiritual forces with which the human race, as a whole, is not well acquainted. You may catch a significant suggestion from this statement: "No two minds ever come together without, thereby, creating a third, invisible, intangible force which may be likened to a third mind."

Keep in mind, there are only two known elements in the whole universe, energy and matter. It is well known that matter may be broken down into units of molecules, atoms, and electrons. There are units of matter that can be isolated, separated, and analyzed. Likewise, there are units of energy. The human mind is a form of energy, a part of it being spiritual in nature. When the minds of two people are coordinated in a SPIRIT OF HARMONY, the spiritual units of energy of each mind form an affinity, which constitutes the "psychic" phase of the Master Mind.

The Master Mind principle, or rather the economic feature of it, was first called to my attention by Andrew Carnegie. Discovery of this principle was responsible for the choice of my life's work. Mr. Carnegie's Master Mind group consisted of a staff of approximately fifty people, with whom he surrounded himself, for the DEFINITE PURPOSE of manufacturing and marketing steel. He attributed his entire fortune to the POWER he accumulated through this "Master Mind."

Analyze the record of anyone who has accumulated a great fortune, and many of those who have accumulated modest fortunes, and you will find that they have either consciously, or unconsciously employed the "Master Mind" principle. GREAT POWER CAN BE ACCUMULATED THROUGH NO OTHER PRINCIPLE! ENERGY is nature's universal set of building blocks, out of which it constructs every material thing in the universe, including human and every form of animal and vegetable life. Through a process that only Nature completely understands, it translates energy into matter.

Nature's building blocks are available to us, in the energy involved in THINKING! The human brain may be compared to an electric battery. It absorbs energy from the ether, which permeates every atom of matter, and fills the entire universe. It is a well known fact that a group of electric batteries will provide more energy than a single battery. It is also a well known fact that an individual battery will provide energy in proportion to the number and capacity of the cells it contains. The brain functions in a similar fashion. This accounts for the fact that some brains are more efficient than others, and leads to this significant statement: a group of brains coordinated (or connected) in a spirit of harmony, will provide more thought-energy than a single brain, just as a group of electric batteries will provide more energy than a single battery.

Through this metaphor, it becomes immediately obvious that the Master Mind principle holds the secret of the POWER wielded by people who surround themselves with other people of brains. There follows, now, another statement which will lead still nearer to an understanding of the psychic phase of the Master Mind principle: When a group of individual brains are coordinated and function in harmony, the increased energy created through that alliance, becomes available to every individual brain in the group.

Henry Ford began his business career under the handicap of poverty, illiteracy, and ignorance. Within the inconceivably short period of ten years, Mr. Ford mastered these three handicaps, and within twenty-five years he made himself one of the richest men in America. Connect with this fact, the additional knowledge that Mr. Ford's most rapid strides became noticeable, from the time he became a personal friend of Thomas A. Edison, and you will begin to understand what the influence of one mind on another can accomplish. Go a step farther, and consider that Mr. Ford's most outstanding achievements began from the time that he formed the acquaintances of Harvey Firestone, John Burroughs, and Luther Burbank (each of great brain capacity), and you will have further evidence that POWER may be produced through the friendly alliance of minds.

There is little if any doubt that Henry Ford was one of the best informed men in the business and industrial world. The question of his wealth needs no discussion.

Analyze Mr. Ford's intimate personal friends, some of whom have already been mentioned, and you will be prepared to understand the following statement: "People take on the nature and the habits and the POWER OF THOUGHT of those with whom they associate in a spirit of sympathy and harmony."

Henry Ford whipped poverty, illiteracy, and ignorance by allying himself with great minds, whose vibrations of thought he absorbed into his own mind. Through his association with Edison, Burbank, Burroughs, and Firestone, Mr. Ford added to his own brain power, the sum and substance of the intelligence, experience, knowledge, and spiritual forces of these four men. Moreover, he appropriated, and made use of the Master Mind principle through the methods of procedure described in this book. *This principle is available to you!*

We have already mentioned Mahatma Gandhi. Perhaps the majority of those who have heard of Gandhi look at him as merely an eccentric little man, who went around without formal clothing, making trouble. In reality, Gandhi was not eccentric, but HE WAS THE MOST POWERFUL MAN OF HIS TIME. (Estimated by the number of followers and their faith in their leader.) In fact, he may be the most powerful man who ever lived. His power was passive, but it was real. How did he attain such stupendous POWER? It may be explained in a few words. He came by POWER by influencing over two hundred million people to coordinate, with mind and body, in a spirit of HARMONY, for a DEFINITE PURPOSE.

In brief, Gandhi accomplished a MIRACLE, for it is a miracle when two hundred million people can be persuaded—not forced—to cooperate in a spirit of HARMONY, for a limitless time. If you doubt that this is a miracle, try to convince ANY TWO PEOPLE to cooperate in a spirit of harmony for *any length of time*. Everyone who manages a business knows what a difficult matter it is to get employees to work together in a spirit even remotely resembling HARMONY.

The list of the chief sources of POWER is headed by INFINITE INTELLIGENCE. When two or more people coordinate in a spirit of HARMONY, and work toward a definite objective, they place themselves in position, through that alliance, to absorb power directly from the great universal storehouse of Infinite Intelligence. This is the greatest of all sources of POWER. It is the source to which the genius turns. It is the source to which every great leader turns, whether conscious of it or not.

The other two major sources of knowledge, necessary for the accumulation of POWER, are no more reliable than the five senses. The senses are not always reliable. Infinite Intelligence DOES NOT ERR. This is not a course on religion. No fundamental principle described in this book should be interpreted as being intended to interfere either directly, or indirectly, with anyone's religious habits. This book has been confined, exclusively, to instructing the reader how to transform the DEFINITE PURPOSE OF DESIRE FOR MONEY, into its monetary equivalent.

Read, *THINK*, and meditate as you read. Soon, the entire subject will unfold, and you will see it in perspective. You are now seeing the detail of the individual chapters. Money is as shy and elusive as the "old time" maiden. It must be wooed and won by methods not unlike those used by a determined lover, in pursuit of the girl of his choice. And, coincidental as it is, the POWER used in the "wooing" of money is not greatly different from that used in wooing a maiden. That power, when successfully used in the pursuit of money must be mixed with FAITH. It must be mixed with DESIRE. It must be mixed with PERSISTENCE. It must be applied through a plan, and that plan must be set into ACTION.

When money comes in quantities known as "the big money," it flows to the one who accumulates it, as easily as water flows down hill. A great unseen stream of POWER exists that could be compared to a river; except that one side flows in one direction, carrying all who get into that side of the stream, onward and upward to WEALTH—and the other side flows in the opposite direction, carrying all who are unfortunate enough to get into it (and not able to extricate themselves from it), downward to misery and POVERTY.

Anyone who has accumulated a great fortune, has witnessed the existence of this stream of life. It consists of one's THINKING PROCESS. The positive emotions of thought form the side of the stream that carries people to fortune. The negative emotions form the side that carries us down to poverty. This carries a thought of stupendous importance to the person who is following this book with the goal of accumulating a fortune. If you are in the side of the stream of POWER that leads to poverty, this may serve as an oar with which to propel yourself over into the other side of the stream. It can serve you ONLY through application and use. Merely reading and passing judgment on it, one way or another, will in no way benefit you.

Some people undergo the experience of alternating between the positive and negative sides of the stream, being at times on the positive side and at times on the negative side. The recent economic collapse has swept millions of people from the positive to the negative side of the stream. These millions are struggling, some of them in desperation and fear, to get back to the positive side of the stream. This book was written especially for those millions.

Poverty and riches often change places. The Crash taught the world this truth, although the world will not long remember the lesson. Poverty may, and generally does, take the place of riches. When riches take the place of poverty, the change is usually brought about through well-conceived and carefully executed PLANS. Poverty needs no plan. It needs no one to aid it, because it is bold and ruthless. Riches are shy and timid. They have to be "attracted."

CHAPTER 10

REDIRECTION OF SEX ENERGY

ANYBODY CAN WISH FOR RICHES, AND MOST PEOPLE DO, BUT ONLY A FEW KNOW THAT A DEFINITE PLAN, PLUS A BURNING DESIRE FOR WEALTH, ARE THE ONLY DEPENDABLE MEANS OF ACCUMULATING WEALTH.

THE MEANING OF the word "redirection" is, in simple language, "the changing, or transferring of one element, or form of energy, into another." The emotion of sex brings into being a state of mind. Because of ignorance on the subject, this state of mind is generally associated with the physical, and because of improper influences, to which most people have been subjected, in acquiring knowledge of sex, things essentially physical have highly biased the mind. The emotion of sex has behind it the possibility of three constructive potentialities, they are:

- The perpetuation of mankind.
- The maintenance of health, (as a therapeutic agency, it has no equal).
- The transformation of mediocrity into genius through redirection.

Sexual redirection is simple and easily explained. It means the switching of the mind from thoughts of physical expression to thoughts of some other nature. Sexual desire is the most powerful of human desires. When driven by this desire, people develop keenness of imagination, courage, will-power, persistence, and creative ability unknown to them at other times. So strong and impelling is the desire for sexual contact that people run the risk of life and reputation to indulge it. When harnessed, and redirected along other lines, this motivating force maintains all of its attributes of keenness of imagination, courage, etc., which may be used as powerful creative forces in literature, art, or in any other profession or calling, including, of course, the accumulation of wealth.

The transformation of sexual energy calls for the exercise of will-power, to be sure, but the reward is worth the effort. The desire for sexual expression is inborn and natural. The desire cannot, and should not be submerged or eliminated. It should be given an outlet through forms of expression that enrich the body, mind, and spirit. If not given this form of outlet, through transformation, it will seek outlets through purely physical channels. A river may be dammed and its water controlled for a time, but eventually, it will force an outlet. The same is true of the emotion of sex. It may be submerged and controlled for a time, but its very nature causes it to be ever seeking means of expression. If it is not directed into some creative effort, it will find a less worthy outlet.

Fortunate, indeed, are people who have discovered how to give sexual emotion an outlet through some creative effort, for they have, by that discovery, lifted themselves to the status of genius. Scientific research has disclosed these significant facts:

- The people of greatest achievement have a highly developed sexual nature; they have learned the art of sexual redirection.
- People, in history, who have accumulated great fortunes and achieved outstanding recognition in literature, art, industry, architecture, and the professions, were often motivated by the influence of someone of the opposite sex.

The research from which these astounding discoveries were made, went back through the pages of biography and history for more than two thousand years. Wherever there was evidence available in connection with the lives of men and women of great achievement, it indicated most convincingly that they possessed highly developed sexual natures. The emotion of sex is an "irresistible force," against which there can be no such opposition as an "immovable body." When driven by this emotion, people become gifted with a super power for action. Understand this, and you will understand how sexual redirection can lift people to the status of genius.

The emotion of sex contains the secret of creative ability. Destroy the sex glands, in humans or animals, and you remove the major source of action. For proof of this, observe what happens to any animal after it has been spayed or neutered. A bull becomes as docile as a cow after it has been altered sexually. Sex alteration takes out the FIGHT.

THE TEN MIND STIMULI

The human mind responds to stimuli, through which it may be "keyed up" to high rates of vibration, known as enthusiasm, creative imagination, intense desire, etc. The stimuli to which the mind responds most freely are:

- The desire for sex expression
- Love
- A burning desire for fame, power, or financial gain, MONEY
- Music
- Friendship between either those of the same sex, or those of the opposite sex.
- A Master Mind alliance based upon the harmony of two or more people who ally themselves for spiritual or temporal advancement.
- Mutual suffering, such as that experienced by people who are persecuted.
- Auto-suggestion
- Fear
- Narcotics and alcohol

The desire for sex expression comes at the head of the list because it most effectively "steps-up" the vibrations of the mind and starts the "wheels" of physical action. Eight of these stimuli are natural and constructive. Two are destructive. The list is presented to enable you to make a comparative study of the major sources of mind stimulation. From this study, it will be readily seen that the emotion of sex is, by great odds, the most intense and powerful of all mind stimuli.

This comparison is proof that redirection of sex energy can lift one to the status of a genius. What exactly constitutes a genius? Some wisecrack has said that a genius is a person who "wears long hair, eats strange food, lives alone, and serves as a target for the joke makers." A better definition of a genius is, *a person who has discovered how to increase the vibrations of thought to the point where they can freely communicate with sources of knowledge not available through the ordinary rate of vibration of thought.*

The person who thinks will question this definition of genius. The first question will be, "How can one communicate with sources of knowledge not available through the ORDINARY rate of vibration of thought?" The next question will be, "Are there known sources of knowledge available only to geniuses, and if so, WHAT ARE THESE SOURCES, and exactly how are they reached?"

GENIUS DEVELOPED THROUGH THE SIXTH SENSE

The reality of a sixth sense has been well established. This sixth sense is Creative Imagination. The power of creative imagination is never used by the majority of people during an entire lifetime, and if used at all, it usually happens by mere accident. A small number of people use, WITH DELIBERATION AND PURPOSE, their creative imaginations. Those who use this power voluntarily, and with understanding of its functions, are GENIUSES. The faculty of creative imagination is the direct link between the finite mind and Infinite Intelligence. All so-called revelations, referred to in religion, and all discoveries of basic or new principles in the field of invention, take place through the creative imagination.

When ideas or concepts flash into your mind, through what is popularly called a "hunch," they come from one or more of the following sources:

- Infinite Intelligence
- One's subconscious mind, wherein is stored every sense impression and thought impulse which ever reached the brain through any of the five senses.
- From the mind of some other person who has just released the thought, or picture of the idea or concept, through conscious thought, or
- From the other person's subconscious storehouse.

CREATIVE IMAGINATION

There are no other KNOWN sources of "inspired" ideas or "hunches." The creative imagination functions best when the mind is vibrating (due to some form of mind stimulation) at an exceedingly high rate. That is, when the mind is functioning at a rate of vibration higher than that of ordinary, normal thought. When brain action is stimulated, through one or more of the ten mind stimulants, it lifts the individual far above the horizon of ordinary thought, and permits them to see distance, scope, and quality of THOUGHTS not available on the lower plane, such as when one is engaged in the solution of the problems of business and professional routine.

When lifted to this higher level of thought, through any form of mind stimulation, the person occupies, relatively, the same position as a person in an airplane, who can see over and beyond the horizon. Moreover, while on this higher level of thought, the person is not hampered or bound by things that limit their vision, such as the necessities of food, clothing, and shelter. They are in a world of thought where ORDINARY, workday thoughts have been removed. While on this exalted plane of THOUGHT, the creative power of the mind is given freedom to act. Once the path has been cleared for the sixth sense to function, it becomes receptive to ideas not available under other circumstances. The sixth sense is the power that marks the difference between a genius and an ordinary person.

The more it is used, the stronger the creative ability becomes. It becomes more alert and receptive to vibrations originating outside the individual's subconscious mind, and the more a person relies on it, and makes demands on it for thought impulses, the stronger it gets. This power of the human mind can be cultivated and developed only through use. That which is known as "conscience" operates entirely through the sixth sense.

The great artists, writers, musicians, and poets become great, because they acquire the habit of relying on that "still, small voice" which speaks from within, through the power of their creative imagination. People who have "keen" imaginations will often tell you that their best ideas come through so-called "hunches." There is a great orator who does not attain to greatness, until he closes his eyes and begins to rely entirely on the faculty of Creative Imagination. When asked why he closed his eyes just before the climaxes of his oratory, he replied, "I do it, because, then I speak through ideas which come to me from within."

One of America's most successful and best known financiers followed the habit of closing his eyes for two or three minutes before making a decision. When asked why he did this, he replied, "With my eyes closed, I am able to draw upon a source of superior intelligence." The late Dr. Elmer R. Gates, of Chevy Chase, Maryland, created more than 200 useful patents, many of them basic, by cultivating and using his creative faculty. His method is both significant and interesting to one interested in attaining the status of genius, in which category Dr. Gates, unquestionably belonged. Dr. Gates was one of the really great, though less publicized scientists of the world.

In his laboratory, he had what he called his "personal communication room." It was practically sound proof, and arranged so that all light could be shut out. It was equipped with a small table, where he kept a pad of paper. In front of the table, on the wall, was the light switch. When Dr. Gates wanted to draw upon the forces available to him through his Creative Imagination, he would go into this room, seat himself at the table, shut off the lights, and CONCENTRATE on the KNOWN factors of the invention he was working on. He would remain in that position until ideas began to "flash" into his mind in connection with the UNKNOWN factors of the invention.

On one occasion, ideas came through so fast that he was forced to write for almost three hours. When the thoughts stopped flowing and he examined his notes, he found they contained a minute description of principles not previously established in the scientific world. The answer to his problem was intelligently presented in those notes. This was how Dr. Gates completed over 200 patents, which had been started, but not completed, by "half-baked" brains. Evidence of the truth of this statement is in the United States Patent Office. Dr. Gates earned his living by "sitting for ideas" for individuals and corporations. Some of the largest corporations in America paid him substantial fees, by the hour, for "sitting for ideas."

The reasoning faculty is often faulty, because it is largely guided by our accumulated experience. Not all knowledge that we accumulate through "experience," is accurate. Ideas received through the creative faculty are much more reliable, for the reason that they come from sources more reliable than any available to the reasoning faculty of the mind. The major difference between the genius and the ordinary mind, may be that the genius works through the faculty of creative imagination, while ordinary people know nothing of this power. The scientific inventor (such as Mr. Edison, and Dr. Gates), makes use of both the synthetic and the creative faculties of imagination.

For example, the scientific inventor, or "genius," begins an invention by organizing and combining the known ideas, or principles accumulated through experience, through the synthetic faculty (the reasoning faculty). If this accumulated knowledge turns out to be insufficient for the completion of an invention, the genius draws on the sources of knowledge available through creative faculty. The exact approach varies with the individual, but this is the sum and substance of the procedure:

- STIMULATE YOUR MIND SO THAT IT VIBRATES ON A HIGHER-THAN-AVERAGE PLANE, using one or more of the ten mind stimulants or some other stimulant of choice.

- CONCENTRATE on the known factors (the finished part) of the problem or situation, and create in your mind a perfect picture of unknown factors (the unfinished part), or solutions to your problem. Hold this picture in your mind until it has been taken over by the subconscious mind, then relax by clearing your mind of ALL thought, and wait for the answer to "flash" into your mind.

Sometimes the results are both definite and immediate. At other times, the results are negative, depending on the state of development of the "sixth sense," or creative faculty.

Mr. Edison tried out more than 10,000 different combinations of ideas through the synthetic faculty of his imagination before he "tuned in" through the creative faculty, and got the answer that perfected the incandescent light. His experience was similar when he produced the talking machine.

Plenty of reliable evidence exists that proves the faculty of creative imagination. This evidence is available through accurate analysis of people who have become leaders in their respective callings, without having had extensive educations. Lincoln was a notable example of a great leader who achieved greatness, through the discovery, and use of his faculty of creative imagination. He discovered, and began to use this faculty as the result of the stimulation of love that he experienced after he met Anne Rutledge, a statement of the highest significance, in connection with the study of the source of genius.

The pages of history are filled with records of great leaders whose achievements may be traced directly to the influence of women who aroused the creative faculties of their minds, through the stimulation of sex desire. Napoleon Bonaparte was one of these. When inspired by his first wife, Josephine, he was irresistible and invincible. When his "better judgment" or reasoning faculty prompted him to put Josephine aside, he began to decline. His defeat and St. Helena were not far distant.

If good taste would permit, we might easily mention scores of men, well known to the American people, who climbed to great heights of achievement under the stimulating influence of their wives, only to drop back to destruction AFTER money and power went to their heads, and they put aside the old wife for a new one. Napoleon was not the only man to discover that sex influence, *from the right source*, is more powerful than any substitute of expediency, which may be created by mere reason.

The human mind responds to stimulation! Among the greatest and most powerful of these stimuli is the urge of sex. When harnessed and transformed, this driving force is capable of lifting us into that higher sphere of thought which enables us to master the sources of worry and petty annoyance. Unfortunately, only the geniuses have made the discovery. Others have accepted the experience of sex urge, without discovering one of its major potentialities—a fact which accounts for the great number of "others" as compared to the limited number of geniuses.

Sex energy is the creative energy of all geniuses. *There never has been, and never will be a great leader, builder, or artist lacking in this driving force of sex.* Surely, no one will misunderstand these statements to mean that ALL who are highly sexed are geniuses! People attain the status of genius ONLY when, and IF, they stimulate their minds to draw upon the forces available, through the creative faculty of the imagination. The biggest source of stimulus for "stepping up" of the vibrations is sex energy. The mere *possession* of this energy is not sufficient to produce a genius. The energy must be *transformed* from desire for physical contact, into some *other* form of desire and action, before it will lift one to the status of a genius.

Far from becoming geniuses, because of great sex desires, the majority of people *lower* themselves, through misunderstanding and misuse of this great force, to the status of the lower animals.

WHY PEOPLE SELDOM SUCCEED BEFORE FORTY

I discovered, from the analysis of over 25,000 people, that people who succeed in an outstanding way, seldom do so before the age of forty, and more often they do not strike their real pace until they are well beyond the age of fifty. This fact was so astounding that it prompted me to go into the study of its cause most carefully, carrying the investigation over a period of more than twelve years.

This study revealed that the major reason why the majority of people who succeed do not begin to do so before the age of forty to fifty, is their tendency to

THINK AND GROW RICH

DISSIPATE their energies through over indulgence in physical expression of the emotion of sex. The majority of people *never* learn that the urge of sex has other possibilities, which far transcend in importance, the mere physical expression. The majority of those who make this discovery, do so *after having wasted many years* at a period when the sex energy is at its height, prior to the age of forty-five to fifty. This usually is followed by noteworthy achievement.

The lives of many people up to, and sometimes well past the age of forty, reflect a continued dissipation of energies, which could have been more profitably turned into better channels. Their finer and more powerful emotions are sown wildly to the four winds. Out of this habit grew the term, "sowing your wild oats." The desire for sexual expression is by far the strongest and most impelling of all the human emotions, and for this very reason this desire, when *harnessed and transformed* into action, other than that of physical expression, can raise a person to the status of a genius.

History is not lacking in examples of people who attained to the status of geniuses, as the result of artificial mind stimulants in the form of alcohol and narcotics. Edgar Allen Poe wrote the "Raven" while under the influence of liquor, "dreaming dreams that mortal never dared to dream before." James Whitcomb Riley did his best writing while under the influence of alcohol. Perhaps it was then he saw "the ordered intermingling of the real and the dream, the mill above the river, and the mist above the stream." Robert Burns wrote best when intoxicated, "For Auld Lang Syne, my dear, we'll take a cup of kindness yet, for Auld Lang Syne."

But let it be remembered that many such people destroyed themselves in the end. Nature has prepared its own potions for people to safely stimulate their minds so they vibrate on a plane that enables them to tune in to fine and rare thoughts which come from—no one knows where! No satisfactory substitute for nature's stimulants has ever been found. It is a fact well known to psychologists that there is a very close relationship between sex desires and spiritual urges—a fact that accounts for the peculiar behavior of people who participate in the orgies known as religious "revivals," common among primitive civilizations.

The world is ruled, and the destiny of civilization is established, by human emotions. People are influenced not by reason so much as by "feelings." The creative faculty of the mind is set into action entirely by emotions, and *not by cold reason*. The most powerful of all human emotions is that of sex. There are other mind stimulants, some of which have been listed, but no one of them, nor all of them combined, can equal the driving power of sex. A mind stimulant is any influence that will temporarily or permanently increase the vibrations of thought. The ten major stimulants, described, are those most commonly resorted to. Through these sources one may commune with Infinite Intelligence, or enter, at will, the storehouse of the subconscious mind, either one's own, or that of another person, a work *of genius*.

A teacher, who has trained and directed the efforts of more than 30,000 sales people, made the astounding discovery that highly sexed individuals are the most efficient salespeople. The explanation is, that the factor of personality known as "personal magnetism" is nothing more or less than sex energy. Highly sexed people always have a plentiful supply of magnetism. Through cultivation and understanding, this vital force may be drawn upon and used to great advantage in the relationships between people.

When hiring salespeople, the capable sales manager looks for the quality of personal magnetism as the *first requirement*. People who lack sex energy will never become enthusiastic or inspire others with enthusiasm, and enthusiasm is one of the most important requisites in sales, no matter what you are selling.

The public speaker, orator, preacher, lawyer, or salesperson who is lacking in sex energy is a "flop," as far as influencing others is concerned. Couple with this, that most people can be influenced only through an appeal to their emotions, and you will understand the importance of sex energy as a part of the salesperson's native ability. Master salespeople attain the status of mastery in selling, because they, either consciously, or unconsciously, *transform* the energy of sex into SALES ENTHUSIASM! In this statement is a very practical suggestion to the actual meaning of sex transformation.

Salespeople who knows how to take their minds off the subject of sex, and direct it in sales effort with as much enthusiasm and determination as they would apply to its original purpose, have acquired the art of sex redirection, whether they know it or not. The majority of salespeople who transform their sex energy do so without being aware of what they are doing, or how they are doing it. Transformation of sex energy calls for more will power than the average person cares to use for this purpose.

CREATING PERSONAL MAGNETISM

Personal magnetic energy can be communicated to others very easily in five simple ways:

The hand-shake. The touch of the hand indicates, instantly, the presence of magnetism, or the lack of it.

Tone of voice. Magnetism, or sex energy, affects the voice and can make it charming and almost musical.

Posture and body language. Highly sexed people move briskly, and with grace and ease.

Vibrations of thought. Highly sexed people mix the emotion of sex with their thoughts, or can do so at will, and in that way, can influence those around them.

Body adornment. People who are highly sexed are usually careful about their personal appearance. They usually select clothing of a style becoming to their personality, physique, complexion, etc.

Those who find it difficult to summon enough will-power for redirection, may gradually acquire the ability. Though this requires will-power, the reward for the practice is more than worth the effort.

The majority of people appear to be unpardonably ignorant of the entire subject of sex. The urge of sex has been grossly misunderstood, slandered, and burlesqued by the ignorant and the evil minded, for so long that the very word sex is seldom used in polite society. Men and women who are known to be blessed—yes, BLESSED—with highly sexed natures, are usually called cursed when they should be called blessed. Millions of people, even in this age of enlightenment, have inferiority complexes because of this false belief that a highly sexed nature is a curse. These statements, of the virtue of sex energy, should not be construed as justification for the womanizer or other indulgent types. The emotion of sex is a virtue ONLY when used intelligently and with discrimination. It may be misused, and often is, to such an extent that it debases, instead of enriches, both body and mind. The better use of this power is the burden of this chapter.

Over-indulgent sex habits are just as detrimental as over-indulgent drinking and eating. In this age in which we live, over-indulgence in habits of sex is common. This orgy of indulgence may account for the shortage of great leaders. People cannot access their creative imaginations while dissipating them. We are the only creature on earth that violates nature's purpose in this connection. Every other animal indulges its sex nature in moderation, and with purpose that harmonizes with the laws of nature. Every other animal responds to the call of sex only in "season." Our inclination is to declare "open season."

Every intelligent person knows that stimulation in excess, through alcoholic drink and narcotics, is a form of addiction that destroys the vital organs of the body, including the brain. Not every person knows, however, that over indulgence in sex expression may become a habit as destructive and as detrimental to creative effort as narcotics or liquor. A sex addict is not essentially different than a drug addict! Both have lost control over their faculties of reason and will-power. Sexual overindulgence can not only destroy reason and willpower, it can also lead to temporary or permanent insanity. Many cases of hypochondria (imaginary illness) grow out of habits developed in ignorance of the true function of sex. From these brief references to the subject, it may be readily seen that ignorance on the subject of sex redirection, forces enormous penalties on the ignorant on the one hand, and withholds from them equally large benefits, on the other.

Widespread ignorance on the subject of sex is due the subject having been surrounded with mystery and clouded in dark silence. The conspiracy of mystery and silence has had the same effect on the minds of young people that the psychology of prohibition had. The result has been increased curiosity and desire to acquire more of this "forbidden" subject; and to the shame of all lawmakers and most physicians-- by training the best qualified to educate youth on that subject--information has not been easily available.

THE MAGIC NUMBER

Seldom does an individual embark on a highly creative effort in any field before the age of forty. The average person reaches the period of their greatest capacity to create between forty and sixty. These statements are based on analysis of thousands of men and women who have been carefully observed. They should be encouraging to those who fail to arrive before the age of forty, and to those who become frightened at the approach of "old age," around the forty-year mark. The years between forty and fifty are, as a rule, the most fruitful. People should approach this age, not with fear and trembling, but with hope and eager anticipation.

If you want evidence that most people do not begin to do their best work before the age of forty, study the records of the most successful people known to America, and you will find it. Henry Ford had not "hit his pace" of achievement until he had passed the age of forty. Andrew Carnegie was well past forty before he began to reap the reward of his efforts. James J. Hill was still running a telegraph key at the age of forty. His stupendous achievements took place after that age. Biographies of American industrialists and financiers are filled with evidence that the period from forty to sixty is the most productive age.

Between the ages of thirty and forty, we begin to learn (if we ever learn), the art of sex transformation. This discovery is generally accidental, and more often than otherwise, people who make it are totally unconscious of their discovery. They will observe that their powers of achievement have increased around the age of thirty-five to forty, but in most cases, they are not familiar with the cause of this change. Nature begins to harmonize the emotions of love and sex in the individual, between the ages of thirty and forty, so that we may draw on these great forces, and apply them jointly as provocation to action.

The emotions are states of mind. Nature has provided us with a "chemistry of the mind" which operates in a manner similar to the principles of chemistry of matter. It is well known that, through chemistry, a chemist can create a deadly poison by mixing certain elements, none of which are—in themselves—harmful in the right proportions. The emotions can also combine to create a deadly poison. The emotions of sex and jealousy, when mixed, can drive a person crazy. The presence of any one or more of the destructive emotions in the human mind, through the chemistry of the mind, sets up a poison that can destroy one's sense of justice and fairness. In extreme cases, the presence of any combination of these emotions in the mind can destroy reason.

ON THE ROAD AGAIN

The road to genius consists of the development, control, and use of sex, love, and romance. Briefly, the process may be stated as follows:

Encourage the presence of these emotions as the dominating thoughts in your mind, and discourage the presence of all the destructive emotions. The mind is a creature of habit. It thrives on the *dominating* thoughts fed to it. Through will-power, you can discourage the presence of any emotion, and encourage the presence of any other. Control of the mind, through the power of will, is not difficult. Control comes from persistence and habit. The secret of control lies in understanding the process of transformation. When any negative emotion presents itself in your mind, it can be transformed into a positive or constructive emotion by simply changing your thoughts.

THERE IS NO OTHER ROAD TO GENIUS THAN THROUGH VOLUNTARY SELF EFFORT! People can reach great heights of financial or business achievement, solely by the driving force of sex energy, but history is filled with evidence that they may, and usually do, carry with them certain traits of character that rob them of the ability to either hold, or enjoy their fortunes. This is worthy of analysis, thought, and meditation, for it states a truth. Ignorance of this has cost thousands of people their privilege of HAPPINESS, even though they possessed riches.

LOVE AND SEX

The emotions of love and sex leave their unmistakable marks on the features. Moreover, these signs are so visible, that all who wish can read them. Those who are driven by the storm of passion, based on sexual desires alone, plainly advertises that fact to the entire world, by the expression of their eyes, and the lines on their face. The emotion of love, when mixed with the emotion of sex, softens, modifies, and beautifies the facial expression. No character analyst is needed to tell you this—you can see it yourself.

The emotion of love brings out, and develops, the artistic and the aesthetic nature of people. It leaves its impression on the soul, even after the fire has been subdued by time and circumstance. Memories of love never pass. They linger, guide, and influence long after the source of stimulation has faded. There is nothing new in this. Every person, who has been moved by GENUINE LOVE, knows that it leaves enduring traces on the human heart. The effect of love endures, because love is spiritual in nature. Those who cannot be lifted to great heights of achievement by love, are hopeless—they are dead, though they may seem to live.

Even the memories of love are sufficient to lift one to a higher plane of creative effort. The major force of love may spend itself and pass away, like a fire that has burned itself out, but it leaves behind indelible marks as evidence that it passed that way. Its departure often prepares the human heart for a still greater love. Go back into your yesterdays, at times, and bathe your mind in the beautiful memories of past love. It will soften the influence of the present worries and annoyances. It will give you a source of escape from the unpleasant realities of life, and maybe—who knows— your mind will yield to you, during this temporary retreat into the world of fantasy, ideas, or plans which could change the entire financial or spiritual status of your life.

If you believe yourself unfortunate, because you have "loved and lost," perish the thought. One who has loved truly, can never lose entirely. Love is whimsical and temperamental. Its nature is ephemeral and transitory. It comes when it pleases and goes away without warning. Accept and enjoy it while it remains, but spend no time worrying about its departure. Worry will never bring it back. Dismiss, also, the thought that love only comes once. Love may come and go, times without number, but there are no two love experiences which affect one in the same way. There may be, and there usually is, one love experience which leaves a deeper imprint on the heart than all the others, but all love experiences are beneficial, except to the person who becomes resentful and cynical when love makes its departure.

There should be no disappointment over love, and there would be none if people understood the difference between the emotions of love and sex. The major difference is that love is spiritual, while sex is biological. No experience, which touches the human heart with a spiritual force, can possibly be harmful, except through ignorance or jealousy. Love is, without question, life's greatest experience. It brings one into communion with Infinite Intelligence. When mixed with the emotions of romance and sex, it may lead one far up the ladder of creative effort. The emotions of love, sex, and romance, are sides of the eternal triangle of achievement-building genius. Nature creates geniuses through no other force.

Love is an emotion with many sides, shades, and colors. The love which one feels for parents or children is quite different from that which one feels for one's sweetheart. The one is mixed with the emotion of sex, while the other is not. The love one feels in true friendship is not the same as that felt for one's sweetheart, parents, or children, but it, too, is a form of love. Then, there is the emotion of love for things inanimate, such as the love of nature. But the most intense and burning of all these various kinds of love is that experienced in the blending of the emotions of love and sex. Marriages, not blessed with the eternal affinity of love, properly balanced and proportioned, with sex, cannot be happy ones—and seldom endure. Love, alone, will not bring happiness in marriage, nor will sex alone. When these two beautiful emotions are blended, marriage may bring about a state of mind, closest to the spiritual that can ever be known on this earthly plane.

When the emotion of romance is added to those of love and sex, the obstructions between the finite mind and Infinite Intelligence are removed. Then a genius has been born! What a different story is this, than those usually associated with the emotion of sex. Here is an interpretation of the emotion that lifts it out of the commonplace and makes it potter's clay in the hands of God, from which He fashions all that is beautiful and inspiring.

CHAPTER 11

THE SUBCONSCIOUS MIND

THE CONNECTING LINK

THE SUBCONSCIOUS MIND is a field of consciousness, where every impulse of thought that reaches the objective mind through any of the five senses, is classified and recorded, and from where thoughts may be recalled or withdrawn as letters may be taken from a filing cabinet. It receives, and files, sense impressions or thoughts, regardless of their nature. You may VOLUNTARILY plant in your subconscious mind any plan, thought, or purpose which you desire to translate into its physical or monetary equivalent. The subconscious acts first on the dominating desires that have been mixed with emotional feeling, such as faith. Consider this in connection with the instructions given in the chapter on DESIRE, for taking the six steps outlined there, and the instructions given in the chapter on the building and execution of plans, and you will understand the importance of the thought conveyed.

THE SUBCONSCIOUS MIND WORKS DAY AND NIGHT. It draws on the forces of Infinite Intelligence for the power with which it voluntarily transforms our desires into their physical equivalent, making use, always of the most practical media by which this end may be accomplished. You cannot *entirely* control your subconscious mind, but you can voluntarily hand it any plan, desire, or purpose you wish transformed into concrete form. There is plenty of evidence to support the belief that the subconscious mind is the connecting link between the finite mind and Infinite Intelligence. We can draw on the forces of Infinite Intelligence at will through this intermediary. It, alone, contains the secret process by which mental impulses are modified and changed into their spiritual equivalent. It, alone, is the medium through which prayer can be transmitted to the source capable of answering prayer.

The possibilities of creative effort connected with the subconscious mind are stupendous and imponderable. They inspire one with awe. I never approach the discussion of the subconscious mind without a feeling of littleness and inferiority due, perhaps, to the fact that our entire stock of knowledge on this subject is so pitifully limited. The very fact that the subconscious mind is the medium of communication between the thinking mind and Infinite Intelligence is, of itself, a thought which almost paralyzes one's reason.

After you have accepted, as a reality, the existence of the subconscious mind, and understand its possibilities, as a medium for transforming your DESIRES into their physical or monetary equivalent, you will comprehend the full significance of the instructions given in the chapter on DESIRE. You will also understand why you have been repeatedly instructed to MAKE YOUR DESIRES CLEAR, AND TO REDUCE THEM TO WRITING. You will also understand the necessity of PERSISTENCE in carrying out instructions. The thirteen principles are the catalyst to help you reach and influence your subconscious mind. Do not become discouraged if you can't do this on the first attempt. Remember that the subconscious mind can only be directed *through habit*, under the directions given in the chapter on FAITH. If you have not yet had time to master faith, be patient. Be persistent.

A good many statements in the chapters on faith and auto-suggestion will be repeated here, for the benefit of YOUR subconscious mind. Remember, your subconscious mind functions voluntarily, *whether you make any effort to influence it or not*. This, naturally, suggests to you that thoughts of fear and poverty, and all negative thoughts serve as suggestions to your subconscious mind, unless, you master these impulses and give it more desirable food to feed on. The subconscious mind will not remain idle! If you fail to plant DESIRES in your subconscious mind, it will feed on the thoughts which reach it as the *result of your neglect*. We have already explained that thought impulses, both negative and positive, are reaching the subconscious mind continuously, from the four sources mentioned in the chapter on Sex Redirection.

For now, it is sufficient if you remember that you are living *daily*, in the midst of all thought impulses, which are reaching your subconscious mind without your knowledge. Some of these impulses are negative, some are positive. You are now engaged in trying to help shut off the flow of negative impulses, and to aid in voluntarily influencing your subconscious mind through positive impulses of DESIRE. When you achieve this, you will possess the key that unlocks the door to your subconscious mind. Moreover, you will control that door so completely, that no undesirable thought can influence your subconscious mind.

Everything we create, BEGINS in the form of a thought impulse. We can create nothing we do not first conceive in THOUGHT. Through the aid of the imagination, thought impulses may be assembled into plans. The imagination, when under control, may be used for the creation of plans or purposes that lead to success in a chosen occupation. All thought impulses, intended for transformation into their physical equivalent, voluntarily planted in the subconscious mind, must pass through the imagination and be mixed with faith. The "mixing" of faith with a plan, or purpose, intended for the subconscious mind, may be done ONLY through the imagination. From these statements, you will notice that voluntary use of the subconscious mind calls for coordination and application of all the principles.

Ella Wheeler Wilcox gave evidence of her understanding of the power of the subconscious mind when she wrote:

> You never can tell what a thought will do
> In bringing you hate or love—
> For thoughts are things, and their airy wings
> Are swifter than carrier doves.
> They follow the law of the universe—
> Each thing creates its kind,
> And they speed O'er the track to bring you back
> Whatever went out from your mind.

Mrs. Wilcox understood the truth: thoughts that go out from one's mind, also imbed themselves deeply in the subconscious mind, where they serve as a magnet, pattern, or blueprint that influences the subconscious mind, translating them into their physical equivalent. Thoughts are truly things, for the reason that every material thing begins in the form of thought-energy. The subconscious mind is more susceptible to influence by impulses of thought mixed with "feeling" or emotion, than by those originating solely in the reasoning portion of the brain. In fact, there is evidence to support the theory, that ONLY emotionalized thoughts have ACTION influence on the subconscious mind. It is well known that emotion or feeling rules the majority of people. If it is true that the subconscious mind responds more quickly to, and is influenced more readily by thought impulses that are well mixed with emotion, it is essential to become familiar with the more important emotions. There are seven major positive emotions, and seven major negative emotions. The negatives voluntarily inject themselves into the thought impulses, which insure passage into the subconscious mind. The positives must be injected, through the principle of auto-suggestion, into the thought impulses which an individual wishes to pass on to the subconscious mind. (Instructions have been given in the chapter on auto-suggestion.)

These emotions, or feeling impulses, may be likened to yeast in a loaf of bread, because they constitute the ACTION element, which transforms thought impulses from the passive to the active state. You are preparing yourself to influence and control the "inner audience" of your subconscious mind, in order to hand over to it the DESIRE for money, which you want transformed into its monetary equivalent. It is essential, therefore, that you understand how to approach this "inner audience." You must speak its language, or it will not hear you. It understands the language of emotion or feeling. Listed below are the seven major positive emotions, and the seven major negative emotions. Your goal should be to draw on the positives and avoid the negatives, when giving instructions to your subconscious mind.

THE SEVEN MAJOR POSITIVE EMOTIONS
DESIRE
FAITH
LOVE
SEX
ENTHUSIASM
ROMANCE
HOPE

There are other positive emotions, but these are the seven most powerful, and the ones most commonly used in creative effort. Master these seven emotions (they can be mastered only by USE), and the other positive emotions will be at your command when you need them. Remember, in this connection, that you are reading a book intended to help you develop a "money consciousness" by *filling your mind with positive emotions*. One does not become money conscious by filling one's mind with negative emotions.

THE SEVEN MAJOR NEGATIVE EMOTIONS (To be avoided)
FEAR
JEALOSY
HATRED
REVENGE
GREED
SUPERSITION
ANGER

Positive and negative emotions cannot occupy the mind at the same time. One or the other must dominate. It is your responsibility to make sure that positive emotions constitute the dominating influence of your mind. Here the law of HABIT will come to your aid. *Form the habit of applying and using the positive emotions!* Eventually, they will dominate your mind so completely, that the negatives *cannot enter it.* Only by following these instructions literally, and continuously, can you gain control over your subconscious mind. The presence of a single negative in your conscious mind is sufficient to *destroy* all chances of constructive aid from your subconscious mind.

If you are an observant person, you have noticed that most people resort to prayer ONLY after everything else has FAILED! Or else they pray by a ritual of meaningless words. And, because most people who pray, do so ONLY AFTER EVERYTHING ELSE HAS FAILED, they go to prayer with their minds filled with FEAR and DOUBT, *which are emotions that the subconscious mind acts on*, and passes on to Infinite Intelligence. Likewise, that is the emotion that Infinite Intelligence receives, and ACTS ON. If you pray for a thing, but have fear as you pray, that you may not receive it, or that your prayer will not be acted on by Infinite

Intelligence, your prayer *will have been in vain*. Prayer does, sometimes, result in the realization of that for which one prays. If you have ever received what you prayed for, go back in your memory, and recall your actual STATE OF MIND, while you were praying, and you will know, for sure, that the theory here described is more than a theory.

Eventually, schools and educational institutions of the country will teach the "science of prayer." Moreover, then prayer may be, and will be reduced to a science. When that time comes, (it will come as soon as we are ready for it, and demand it), no one will approach the Universal Mind in a state of fear, for the very good reason that there will be no such emotion as fear. Ignorance, superstition, and false teaching will have disappeared, and we will have attained the true status of children of Infinite Intelligence. A few have already attained this blessing. If you believe this prophesy is far-fetched, take a look at the human race in retrospect. Less than a hundred years ago, people believed the lightning was the wrath of God, and feared it. Now, thanks to the power of FAITH, we have harnessed the lightning and made it turn the wheels of industry. Much less than a hundred years ago, we believed the space between the planets to be nothing but a great void, a stretch of dead nothingness. Now, thanks to this same power of FAITH, we know that far from being either dead or a void, the space between the planets is very much alive, that it is the highest form of vibration known, excepting, perhaps, the vibration of THOUGHT. Moreover, we know that this living, pulsating, vibratory energy, which permeates every atom of matter and fills every niche of space, connects every human brain with every other human brain.

What reason do we have not to believe that this same energy connects every human brain with Infinite Intelligence? There are no toll-gates between the finite mind and Infinite Intelligence. The communication costs nothing except Patience, Faith, Persistence, Understanding, and a SINCERE DESIRE to communicate. Moreover, the approach can be made only by the individual himself. Paid prayers are worthless. Infinite Intelligence does no business by proxy. You either go direct or you do not communicate. You can buy prayer books and repeat them until the day you die, without avail. Thoughts you wish to communicate to Infinite Intelligence, must undergo transformation, which happens only through your own subconscious mind. The method by which you can communicate with Infinite Intelligence is very similar to how the vibration of sound is communicated by radio. If you understand the working principle of radio, you of course, know that sound cannot be communicated through the ether until it has been "stepped up," or changed into a rate of vibration that the human ear cannot detect. The radio sending station picks up the sound of the human voice, and "scrambles," or modifies it by stepping up the vibration millions of times. Only in this way, can the vibration of sound be communicated through the ether. After this transformation has taken place, the ether "picks up" the energy (which originally was in the form of vibrations of sound), carries that energy to radio receiving stations, and these receiving sets "step" that energy back down to its original rate of vibration so it is recognized as sound.

The subconscious mind is the intermediary that translates our prayers into terms the Infinite Intelligence can recognize, presents the message, and brings back the answer in the form of a definite plan or idea for procuring the object of the prayer. Understand this principle, and you will know why mere words read from a prayer book cannot, and will never serve as an agency of communication between the mind of man and Infinite Intelligence. Before your prayer will reach Infinite Intelligence (a statement of the author's theory only), it probably is transformed from its original thought vibration into terms of spiritual vibration. Faith is the only known agency that will give your thoughts a spiritual nature. FAITH and FEAR make poor bedfellows. *Where one is found, the other cannot exist.*

CHAPTER 12

THE BRAIN

A BROADCASTING AND RECEIVING STATION FOR THOUGHT

EVERY HUMAN BRAIN is both a broadcasting and receiving station for the vibration of thought. Through the medium of the ether, in a fashion similar to that employed by the radio broadcasting principle, every human brain is capable of picking up vibrations of thought which are being released by other brains.

In connection with the statement in the preceding paragraph, compare, and consider the description of the Creative Imagination, outlined in the chapter on Imagination. The Creative Imagination is the "receiving set" of the brain, which receives thoughts released by the brains of others. It is the agency of communication between one's conscious, or reasoning mind, and the four sources from which one may receive thought provocation. When stimulated, or "stepped up" to a high rate of vibration, the mind becomes more receptive to the vibration of thought that reaches it. This "stepping up" process takes place through the positive emotions, or the negative emotions. Through emotion, the vibrations of thought may be increased. Vibrations of an exceedingly high rate are the only vibrations picked up and carried from one brain to another. Thought is energy travelling at an exceedingly high rate of vibration. Thought, which has been modified or "stepped up" by any of the major emotions, vibrates at a much higher rate than ordinary thought, and it is this type of thought that passes from one brain to another, through the broadcasting machinery of the human brain.

The emotion of sex stands at the head of the list of human emotions, as far as intensity and driving force are concerned. The brain that has been stimulated by the emotion of sex, vibrates at a much more rapid rate than it does when that emotion is dormant or absent. Sex transmutations increase the rate of vibration of thoughts to such a pitch that the Creative Imagination becomes highly receptive to ideas available in the ether. On the other hand, when the brain is vibrating at a rapid rate, it not only attracts thoughts and ideas released by other brains, it gives to one's own thoughts that "feeling" which is essential before those thoughts will be picked up and acted on by the subconscious mind.

The broadcasting principle is the way you mix feeling, or emotion, with your thoughts and pass them on to your subconscious mind. The subconscious mind is the "sending station" of the brain, where vibrations of thought are broadcast. The Creative Imagination is the "receiving set," through which the vibrations of thought are picked up. Through the instructions described in the chapter on auto-suggestion, you were definitely informed of the method by which DESIRE may be transformed into its monetary equivalent.

Operation of your mental "broadcasting" station is a comparatively simple procedure. You have three principles to bear in mind, and to apply, when you wish to use your broadcasting station: the SUBCONSCIOUS MIND, CREATIVE IMAGINATION, and AUTO-SUGGESTION. The way you put these three principles into action has been described. The procedure begins with DESIRE.

THE GREATEST FORCES ARE "INTANGIBLE"

The economic collapse brought the world to the very border-line of understanding of the intangible and unseen forces. In the past, we have depended too much on our physical senses, and have limited our knowledge to physical things, which we could see, touch, weigh, and measure. We are now entering the most marvelous of all ages—an age that will teach us something of the intangible forces of the world around us. Perhaps we will learn, as we pass through this age, that the "other self" is more powerful than the physical self we see when we look into a mirror.

Occasionally, people will speak lightly of the intangibles—the things they cannot perceive through any of their five senses, and when we hear them, it should remind us that *all of us are controlled by forces unseen and intangible.* Not even the whole of mankind has the power to cope with or to control the intangible force wrapped up in the rolling waves of the oceans. We don't have the capacity to understand the intangible force of gravity, which keeps this little earth suspended in mid-air, and keeps us from falling from it, much less the power to control that force. We are entirely subservient to the intangible force that comes with a hurricane, and we are just as helpless in the presence of the intangible force of electricity—We don't even know what electricity is, where it comes from, or what its purpose is! We do not understand the intangible force (and intelligence) wrapped up in the soil of the earth—*the force that provides us with every morsel of food we eat, every article of clothing we wear, every dollar we carry in our pocket.*

THE DRAMATIC STORY OF THE BRAIN

Last, but not least, man, with all of our boasted culture and education, understands little or nothing of the intangible force (the greatest of all the intangibles) of *thought.* We know little about the physical brain, and its vast network of intricate machinery through which the power of thought is translated into its material equivalent, but we are entering an age that will yield enlightenment on the subject. It is inconceivable that such a network of intricate machinery should be in existence for the sole purpose of carrying on the physical functions incidental to growth and maintenance of the physical body, otherwise our brains would be much smaller, as they are in the animals. Is it not likely that the same system, which gives billions of brain cells the media for communication one with another, also provides the means of communication with other intangible forces?

Years ago, the New York Times ran an editorial on the invisible powers of the mind. The editorial briefly analyzed the work carried on by Dr. Rhine, and his associates at Duke University.

WHAT IS TELEPATHY?

Some time ago, we cited some of the remarkable results achieved by Professor Rhine and his associates in Duke University from more than a hundred thousand tests to determine the existence of 'telepathy' and 'clairvoyance.' These results were summarized in the first two articles in Harpers Magazine. In the second, which has now appeared, the author, E. H. Wright, attempts to summarize what has been learned, or what it seems reasonable to infer, regarding the exact nature of these 'extrasensory' modes of perception.

The actual existence of telepathy and clairvoyance now seems to some scientists enormously probable as the result of Rhine's experiments. Participants were asked to name as many cards in a special pack as they could without looking at them and without other sensory access to them. About twenty people were discovered who could regularly name so many of the cards correctly that 'there was not one chance in many a million of their having done their feats by luck or accident.'

But how did they do them? These powers, assuming that they exist, do not seem to be sensory. There is no known organ for them. The experiments worked just as well at distances of several hundred miles as they did in the same room. These facts also dispose, in Mr. Wright's opinion, of the attempt to explain telepathy or clairvoyance through any physical theory of radiation. All known forms of radiant energy decline inversely as the distance grows. Telepathy and clairvoyance do not. Contrary to widespread opinion, they do not improve when the participant is asleep or half-asleep, but, on the contrary, when they are most wide-awake and alert. Rhine discovered that a narcotic will invariably lower a person's score, while a stimulant will always send it higher. The most reliable performers apparently cannot make a good score unless they try to do their best.

One conclusion that Wright draws, with some confidence, is that telepathy and clairvoyance are really the same gift. That is, the faculty that 'sees' a card face down on a table seems to be exactly the same one that 'reads' a thought residing only in another mind. There are several grounds for believing this. So far, for example, the two gifts have been found in every person who enjoys either of them. In everyone so far, the two have been of equal vigor, almost exactly. Screens, walls, distances, have no effect at all on either. Wright concludes what he puts forward as no more than a mere 'hunch' that other extra-sensory experiences, prophetic dreams, premonitions of disaster, and the like, may also prove to be part of the same faculty. The reader is not asked to accept any of these conclusions, but the evidence that Rhine has piled up remains impressive.

In view of Dr. Rhine's observations of how the mind responds to what he terms "extra-sensory" perception, I will add to his testimony by stating that my associates and I have discovered the ideal conditions for the mind to be stimulated so that the sixth sense, described in the next chapter, will function in a practical way. The conditions consist of a close working alliance between myself and two members of my staff. Through experimentation and practice, we have discovered how to stimulate our minds (by applying the principle used in connection with the "Invisible Counselors" described in the next chapter) so that we can, by a process of blending our three minds into one, find the solution to a great variety of personal problems submitted by my clients.

The procedure is very simple. We sit down at a conference table, clearly state the nature of the problem, and then begin discussing it. Each contributes whatever thoughts that may occur. The strange thing about this method of mind stimulation is that it places each participant in communication with unknown sources of knowledge outside their own experience. If you understand the principle described in the chapter on the Master Mind, you recognize the round-table "brain-storming" procedure here described as being a practical application of the Master Mind. This method of mind stimulation, through harmonious discussion of definite subjects, between three people, illustrates the simplest and most practical use of the Master Mind.

By adopting and following a similar plan, any student of this philosophy can obtain the famous Carnegie formula briefly described in the introduction. If it means nothing to you at this time, mark this page and read it again after you have finished the last chapter.

CHAPTER 13

THE SIXTH SENSE

THE DOOR TO THE TEMPLE OF WISDOM

THE "DEPRESSION" WAS A BLESSING IN DISGUISE. IT REDUCED THE WHOLE WORLD TO A NEW STARTING POINT THAT GIVES EVERY ONE A NEW OPPORTUNITY.

THE THIRTEENTH PRINCIPLE is known as the SIXTH SENSE. Through this sense, Infinite Intelligence can communicate voluntarily, without any effort from the individual. This principle is the apex of the philosophy. It can be assimilated, understood, and applied ONLY by first mastering the other twelve principles. The SIXTH SENSE is that portion of the subconscious mind referred to as the Creative Imagination. It has also been referred to as the "receiving set" through which ideas, plans, and thoughts flash into the mind. The "flashes" are sometimes called "hunches" or "inspirations."

The sixth sense defies description! It cannot be described to a person who has not mastered the other principles of this philosophy, because such a person has no knowledge, and no experience with which the sixth sense may be compared. Understanding the sixth sense comes only by meditation through mind development *from within*. The sixth sense probably is the medium of contact between the finite mind and Infinite Intelligence, and for this reason, *it is a mixture of both the mental and the spiritual.* It is believed to be the point at which the mind contacts the Universal Mind. After you have mastered the principles described in this book, you will be prepared to accept as truth a statement which may, otherwise, be incredible to you, namely:

Through the aid of the sixth sense, you will be warned of impending dangers in time to avoid them, and notified of opportunities in time to embrace them.

There comes to your aid, and to do your bidding, with the development of the sixth sense, a "guardian angel" who will open to you at all times the door to the Temple of Wisdom. Whether or not this is a statement of truth, you will never know, except by following the instructions described in the pages of this book or some similar method.

I am not a believer in, nor an advocate of "miracles," for the reason that I have enough knowledge of Nature to understand that Nature *never deviates from its established laws*. Some of nature's laws are so incomprehensible that they produce what appear to be "miracles." The sixth sense comes as near to being a miracle as anything I have ever experienced, and it appears so, only because I do not understand how it works. This much I do know: there is a power, or a First Cause, or an Intelligence that permeates every atom of matter and embraces every unit of energy. This Infinite Intelligence converts acorns into oak trees, causes water to flow downhill in response to the law of gravity, follows night with day and winter with summer, each maintaining its proper place and relationship to the other. This Intelligence, through the principles of this philosophy, can transform DESIRES into concrete or material form. I know this because I have experimented with it—and I have EXPERIENCED IT.

Step by step, through the preceding chapters, you have been led to this, the last principle. If you have mastered each of the preceding principles, you are now prepared to accept, *without being skeptical*, the stupendous claims made here. If you have not mastered the other principles, you must do so before you can determine, definitely, whether the claims made in this chapter are fact or fiction. While I was passing through the age of "hero-worship" I found myself trying to imitate those I most admired. Moreover, I discovered that the element of FAITH, with which I used to imitate my idols, gave me great capacity to do so quite successfully. I have never entirely divested myself of this habit of hero-worship, even though I have passed the age where most people give it up. My experience has taught me that the next best thing to being truly great, is to emulate the great, by feeling and action, as much as possible.

Long before I had ever written a line for publication, or endeavored to deliver a speech in public, I followed the habit of reshaping my own character, by trying to imitate the nine people whose lives and life-works had been most impressive to me. These were Emerson, Paine, Edison, Darwin, Lincoln, Burbank, Napoleon, Ford, and Carnegie. Every night, over a long period of years, I held an imaginary Council meeting with this group I called my "Invisible Counselors."

The procedure was this. Just before going to sleep at night, I would shut my eyes and see, in my imagination, this group of men seated with me around my Council Table. Here, I had not only an opportunity to sit among those I considered great, but I actually dominated the group, by serving as the Chairman. I had a very DEFINITE PURPOSE in indulging my imagination through these nightly meetings. My purpose was to rebuild my own character so it would represent a composite of the characters of my imaginary counselors. Realizing, as I did, early in life, that I had to overcome the handicap of birth in an environment of ignorance and superstition, I deliberately assigned myself the task of voluntary rebirth through the method here described.

BUILDING CHARACTER WITH AUTO-SUGGESTION

Being an earnest student of psychology, I knew, of course, that all people have become what they are, because of their DOMINATING THOUGHTS AND DESIRES. I knew that every deeply seated desire has the effect of causing one to seek outward expression for that desire may be transformed into reality. I knew that self-suggestion is a powerful factor in building character, that it is, in fact, the sole principle of character building. With this knowledge of mind operation, I was well armed with the equipment needed in rebuilding my character. In these imaginary Council meetings, I called on my Cabinet members for the knowledge I wished each to contribute, addressing myself to each member, out loud, in the following words:

"Mr. Emerson, I desire to acquire from you the marvelous understanding of nature that distinguished your life. I ask that you make an impression on my subconscious mind, of the qualities you possessed that enabled you to understand and adapt yourself to the laws of nature. I ask that you assist me in reaching and drawing on the sources of knowledge available to this end.

"Mr. Burbank, I request that you pass on to me the knowledge that enabled you to harmonize the laws of nature that you caused the cactus to shed its thorns, and become an edible food. Give me access to the knowledge that enabled you to make two blades of grass grow where none grew before, and helped you to blend the coloring of the flowers with more splendor and harmony, for you, alone, have successfully gilded the lily.

"Napoleon, I desire to acquire from you, by emulation, the marvelous ability you possessed to inspire men, and to arouse them to greater and more determined spirit of action. Also to acquire the spirit of enduring FAITH, which enabled you to turn defeat into victory, and to surmount staggering obstacles. Emperor of Fate, King of Chance, Man of Destiny, I salute you!

"Mr. Paine, I desire to acquire from you the freedom of thought and the courage and clarity to express convictions, which so distinguished you!

"Mr. Darwin, I wish to acquire from you the marvelous patience, and ability to study cause and effect, without bias or prejudice, so exemplified by you in the field of natural science.

"Mr. Lincoln, I desire to build into my own character the keen sense of justice, the untiring spirit of patience, the sense of humor, the human understanding, and the tolerance, which were your distinguishing characteristics.

"Mr. Carnegie, I am already indebted to you for my choice of a life-work, which has brought me great happiness and peace of mind. I wish to acquire a thorough understanding of the principles of *organized effort*, which you used so effectively in the building of a great industrial enterprise.

"Mr. Ford, you have been among the most helpful of the men who have supplied much of the material essential to my work. I wish to acquire your spirit of persistence, the determination, poise, and self-confidence which have enabled you to master poverty, organize, unify, and simplify human effort, so I can help others follow in your footsteps.

"Mr. Edison, I have seated you nearest to me, at my right, because of the personal cooperation you have given me, during my research into the causes of success and failure. I wish to acquire from you the marvelous spirit of FAITH, with which you have uncovered so many of nature's secrets, the spirit of unremitting effort with which you have so often pulled victory from defeat."

My method of addressing the members of the imaginary Cabinet would vary, according to the traits I was most interested in acquiring. I studied the records of their lives with painstaking care. After some months of this nightly procedure, I was astounded by the discovery that these imaginary figures became, apparently *real*. Each of these people developed individual characteristics, which surprised me. For example, Lincoln developed the habit of always being late, then walking around in solemn parade. When he came, he walked very slowly, with his hands clasped behind him, and once in a while, he would stop as he passed, and rest his hand, momentarily, on my shoulder. He always wore an expression of seriousness on his face. Rarely did I see him smile. The cares of a sundered nation made him grave.

That was not true of the others. Burbank and Paine often indulged in witty banter that seemed, at times, to shock the other members of the cabinet. One night Paine suggested that I prepare a lecture on "The Age of Reason," and deliver it from the pulpit of a church I formerly attended. Many around the table laughed heartily at the suggestion. Not Napoleon! He drew his mouth down at the corners and groaned so loudly that all turned and looked at him with amazement. To him, the church was but a pawn of the State, not to be reformed, but to be used as a convenient inciter to mass activity by the people.

On one occasion, Burbank was late. When he came, he was excited with enthusiasm and explained that he was late because of an experiment he was attempting, to grow apples on any sort of tree. Paine chided him by reminding him that it was an apple that started all the trouble between man and woman. Darwin chuckled heartily as he suggested that Paine should watch out for little serpents, when he went into the forest to gather apples, as they had the habit of growing into big snakes. Emerson observed, "No serpents, no apples," and Napoleon remarked, "No apples, no state!"

Lincoln developed the habit of always being the last one to leave the table after each meeting. On one occasion, he leaned across the end of the table, his arms folded, and remained in that position for many minutes. I made no attempt to disturb him. Finally, he lifted his head slowly, got up and walked to the door, then turned around, came back, and laid his hand on my shoulder and said, "My boy, you will need much courage if you remain steadfast in carrying out your purpose in life. But remember, when difficulties overtake you, the common people have common sense. Adversity will develop it."

One evening Edison arrived ahead of all the others. He walked over and seated himself at my left, where Emerson usually sat, and said, "You are destined to witness the discovery of the secret of life. When the time comes, you will observe that life consists of great swarms of energy, or entities, each as intelligent as human beings *think* themselves to be. These units of life group together like hives of bees, and remain together until they disintegrate, *through lack of harmony*. These units have differences of opinion, the same as human beings, and often fight among themselves. These meetings you are conducting will be very helpful to you. They will bring to your rescue some of the same units of life that served the members of your Cabinet, during their lives. These units are eternal. THEY NEVER DIE! Your own thoughts and DESIRES serve as the magnet that attracts units of life, from the great ocean of life out there. Only the friendly units are attracted—the ones that harmonize with the nature of your DESIRES."

The other members of the Cabinet began to enter the room. Edison got up and slowly walked around to his own seat. Edison was still living when this happened. It impressed me so greatly that I went to see him and told him about the experience. He smiled broadly, and said, "Your dream was more a reality than you may imagine it to have been." He added no further explanation to his statement.

These meetings became so realistic that I became fearful of their consequences, and discontinued them for several months. The experiences were so uncanny, I was afraid if I continued them I would lose sight of the fact that the meetings were purely *my imagination*. Some six months after I had discontinued the practice I was awakened one night, or thought I was, when I saw Lincoln standing at my bedside. He said, "The world will soon need your services. It is about to undergo a period of chaos which will cause men and women to lose faith and become panic stricken. Go ahead with your work and complete your philosophy. That is your mission in life. If you neglect it, for any reason, you will be reduced to a primal state and be compelled to retrace the cycles through which you have passed during thousands of years."

I was unable to tell, the following morning, whether I had dreamed this, or had actually been awake, and I have never since found out which it was, but I do know that the dream, if it were a dream, was so vivid in my mind the next day that I resumed my meetings the following night.

At our next meeting, the members of my Cabinet all filed into the room together, and stood at their accustomed places at the Council Table, while Lincoln raised a glass and said, "Gentlemen, let us drink a toast to a friend who has returned to the fold." After that, I began to add new members to my Cabinet, until it consisted of more than fifty, among them Christ, St. Paul, Galileo, Copernicus, Aristotle, Plato, Socrates, Homer, Voltaire, Bruno, Spinoza, Drummond, Kant, Schopenhauer, Newton, Confucius, Elbert Hubbard, Brann, Ingersoll, Wilson, and William James.

This is the first time that I have had the courage to mention this. Up until now, I have remained quiet on the subject, because I knew, from my own attitude in connection with such matters, that I would be misunderstood if I described my unusual experience. I have been emboldened now to reduce my experience to the

THINK AND GROW RICH

printed page, because I am now less concerned about what "they say" than I was in the years that have passed. One of the blessings of maturity is that it sometimes brings greater courage to be truthful, regardless of what those who do not understand, may think or say.

To be clear, I want to state most emphatically, that I regarded my Cabinet meetings as being purely imaginary. However, I feel entitled to say that, while the members of my Cabinet may be purely fictional, and the meetings existed only in my imagination, they led me into glorious paths of adventure, rekindled an appreciation of true greatness, encouraged creative endeavor, and emboldened the expression of honest thought.

Somewhere in the cell-structure of the brain, is located an organ which receives vibrations of thought ordinarily called "hunches." So far, science has not discovered where this organ of the sixth sense is located, but this is not important. The fact remains that human beings do receive accurate knowledge, through sources other than the physical senses. Such knowledge, generally, is received when the mind is under the influence of extraordinary stimulation. Any emergency that arouses the emotions and causes the heart to beat more rapidly than normal, generally brings the sixth sense into action. Anyone who has experienced a near accident while driving, knows that on such occasions, the sixth sense often comes to one's rescue, and aids, by split seconds, in avoiding the accident.

These facts are mentioned preliminary to a statement of the fact that during my meetings with the "Invisible Counselors," I found my mind most receptive to ideas, thoughts, and knowledge that reached me through the sixth sense. I can truthfully say that I owe entirely to my "Invisible Counselors" full credit for such ideas, facts, or knowledge as I received through "inspiration." On scores of occasions, when I have faced emergencies, some of them so grave that my life was in jeopardy, I have been miraculously guided past these difficulties through the influence of my "Invisible Counselors." My original purpose in conducting Council meetings with imaginary beings, was solely that of impressing my own subconscious mind, through the principle of auto-suggestion, with certain characteristics I wanted to acquire. Later, my experimentation took on an entirely different trend. I could go to my imaginary counselors with every difficult problem confronting me or my clients. The results have often been astonishing, although I do not depend entirely on this form of Counsel.

You, of course, have recognized that this chapter covers a subject that most people are not familiar with. The Sixth Sense is a subject that will be of great interest and benefit to the person who aims to accumulate vast wealth, but it is not necessary for those whose desires are more modest. Henry Ford, undoubtedly understood and made practical use of the sixth sense. His vast business and financial operations made it necessary for him to understand and use this principle. Thomas A. Edison understood and used the sixth sense in connection with the development of inventions, especially those involving basic patents, of which he had no human experience and no accumulated knowledge to guide him, as was the case while he was working on the talking machine, and the motion picture machine. Nearly all great leaders, such as Napoleon, Bismarck, Joan of Arc, Christ, Buddha, Confucius, and Mohammed, understood and probably made use of the sixth sense continuously. The major portion of their greatness was in their knowledge of this principle.

The sixth sense is not something that one can turn off and on at will. Ability to use this great power comes slowly, through application of the other principles outlined in this book. Seldom does any individual come into workable knowledge of the sixth sense before the age of forty. More often, the knowledge is not available until one is well past fifty, because the spiritual forces, with which the sixth sense is so closely related, mature and become usable only through years of meditation, self-examination, and serious thought. No matter who you are, or what may have been your purpose in reading this book, you can benefit from it without understanding the principle described in this chapter. This is especially true if your major purpose is accumulating money or other material things.

The chapter on the sixth sense was included, because the book is designed to present a complete philosophy for guiding yourself in attaining whatever you ask of life. The starting point of all achievement is DESIRE. The finishing point is that brand of KNOWLEDGE that leads to understanding—understanding of self, understanding of others, understanding of the laws of nature, recognition and understanding of HAPPINESS. This sort of understanding comes in its fullness only through familiarity with, and use of the principle of the sixth sense, hence that principle had to be included as a part of this philosophy, for the benefit of those who demand more than money.

Having read the chapter, you must have observed that while reading it, you were lifted to a high level of mental stimulation. Splendid! Come back to this again a month from now, read it once more, and observe that your mind will soar to a still higher level of stimulation. Repeat this experience from time to time, giving no concern as to how much or how little you learn at the time, and eventually you will find yourself in possession of a power that will enable you to throw off discouragement, master fear, overcome procrastination, and draw freely on your imagination. Then you will have felt the touch of that unknown "something," which has been the moving spirit of every truly great thinker leader, artist, musician, writer, and statesman. Then you will be in position to transform your DESIRES into their physical or financial counterpart as easily as you can lie down and quit at the first sign of opposition.

FAITH VS. FEAR!

Previous chapters have described how to develop FAITH, through Auto-suggestion, Desire, and the Subconscious. The next chapter presents detailed instructions for the mastery of FEAR. You will find a full description of the six fears that cause all discouragement, timidity, procrastination, indifference, indecision, and lack of ambition, self-reliance, initiative, self-control, and enthusiasm.

THINK AND GROW RICH

Search yourself carefully as you study these six enemies. They may exist only in your subconscious mind, where their presence will be hard to detect. Remember, too, as you analyze the "Six Ghosts of Fear," that they are nothing but ghosts because they exist only in the mind. Remember, also, that ghosts—creations of uncontrolled imagination—have caused most of the damage people have done to their own minds, therefore, ghosts can be as dangerous as if they lived and walked on the earth in physical bodies.

The Ghost of the Fear of Poverty, which seized the minds of millions of people in 1929, was so real that it caused the worst business depression this country has ever known. Moreover, this particular ghost is still alive today, thriving on the recent economic failure.

CHAPTER 14

FIVE GHOSTS OF FEAR

Take Inventory of Yourself, As You Read This Closing Chapter,
and Find out How Many of the "Ghosts" Are Standing in Your Way

BEFORE YOU CAN put any portion of this philosophy to use, your mind must be prepared to receive it. The preparation is not difficult. It begins with study, analysis, and understanding of three enemies that you will have to clear out. These are INDECISION, DOUBT, and FEAR!

The Sixth Sense will never function while these three negatives, or any of them, remain in your mind. The members of this unholy trio are closely related; where one is found, the other two are close at hand. INDECISION is the seedling of FEAR! Remember this, as you read. Indecision crystallizes into DOUBT, the two blend and become FEAR! The "blending" process often is slow. This is one reason why these three enemies are so dangerous. They germinate and grow *without their presence being observed*. This chapter describes an end that must be attained before the philosophy, as a whole, can be put into practical use. It also analyzes a condition that has reduced huge numbers of people to poverty, and it states a truth that must be understood by all who accumulate wealth, whether measured in terms of money or a state of mind of far greater value than money.

The purpose of this chapter is to turn the spotlight of attention on the cause and cure of the six basic fears. Before we can master an enemy, we must know its name, its habits, and where it lives. As you read, analyze yourself carefully and determine which, if any, of the six common fears have attached themselves to you. Do not be deceived by the habits of these subtle enemies. Sometimes they remain hidden in the subconscious mind, where they are difficult to locate, and even more difficult to eliminate.

THE FIVE BASIC FEARS

There are five basic fears that every human suffers, in some combination, at one time or another. Most people are fortunate if they do not suffer from the entire five. In order of their most common appearance, they are:

POVERTY

CRITICISM

ILLNESS

(The first three constitute the basis for most of worries)

OLD AGE

DEATH

All other fears are of minor importance, and can be grouped under these five headings. The prevalence of these fears, as a curse to the world, runs in cycles. For almost six years, while the depression was on, the country floundered in the cycle of FEAR OF POVERTY. During the world-war, we were in the cycle of FEAR OF DEATH. Just following the war, we were in the cycle of FEAR OF ILL HEALTH, as evidenced by the epidemic of disease that spread itself all over the world. In recent times, we have seen a repeat of this cycle in a different order. After 9/11, the fear of DEATH; after avian flu and swine flu, the fear of ILLNESS; and after the economic collapse, a fear of POVERTY.

Fears are nothing more than states of mind. Our state of mind can be controlled and directed. Physicians, as everyone knows, are less subject to attack by disease than ordinary people, because they DO NOT FEAR DISEASE. Physicians, without fear or hesitation, physically contact hundreds of people, weekly, who are suffering from contagious illnesses, without becoming infected. Their immunity against the disease consists, largely, in their absolute lack of FEAR.

We can create nothing that we do not first conceive in the form of an impulse of thought. Following this statement, comes another of still greater importance, namely, THOUGHT IMPULSES BEGIN IMMEDIATELY TO TRANSLATE THEMSELVES INTO THEIR PHYSICAL EQUIVALENT, WHETHER THOSE THOUGHTS ARE VOLUNTARY OR INVOLUNTARY. Thought impulses that are picked up through the ether, by mere chance (thoughts that have been released by other minds) can determine a person's financial, business, professional, or social destiny just as surely as do the thought impulses that are created intentionally.

This is important for those who do not understand why some people appear to be "lucky" while others of equal or greater ability, training, experience, and brain capacity, seem destined to ride with misfortune. This can be explained by the statement that *every human being has the ability to completely control his own mind*, and with this control, obviously, every person may open their minds to lower thought impulses that are released by other brains, or close the doors tightly and admit only thought impulses of their own choosing. Nature has endowed us with absolute control over only one thing, and that is THOUGHT. This fact, coupled with the additional fact that everything we create, begins in the form of a thought, leads us to the principle of mastering FEAR.

If it is true that ALL THOUGHT HAS A TENDENCY TO CLOTHE ITSELF IN ITS PHYSICAL EQUIVALENT (and this is true, beyond any reasonable doubt), it is equally true that thought impulses of fear and poverty cannot be translated into terms of courage and financial gain. The people of America began to think of poverty, following the Wall Street crash of 1929. Slowly, but surely that mass thought was crystallized into its physical equivalent, which was known as the "great depression." This had to happen; it is in conformity with the laws of nature. Again, we are seeing this phenomenon after the crash of 2008. Unless we can overcome our fear, as a nation, we will again experience a great depression. This time is, however, presents an opportunity for unafraid individuals to reap rewards and find success that the rest of the population cannot even recognize through the fog of FEAR.

THE FEAR OF POVERTY

There can be no compromise between POVERTY and RICHES! The two roads that lead to poverty and riches travel in opposite directions. If you want riches, you must refuse to accept any circumstance that leads toward poverty. (The word "riches" is here used in its broadest sense, meaning financial, spiritual, mental, and material wealth). The starting point of the path that leads to riches is DESIRE. In chapter one, you received full instructions for the proper use of DESIRE. In this chapter, you have complete instructions for preparing your mind to make practical use of DESIRE.

Here, then, is the place to give yourself a challenge that will definitely determine how much of this philosophy you absorbed. Here is the point where you become a prophet and foretell, accurately, what the future holds for you. If, after reading this chapter, you are willing to accept poverty, you may as well make up your mind to receive poverty. This is one decision you cannot avoid. If you demand riches, determine what form, and how much will be required to satisfy you. You know the road that leads to riches. You have been given a road map that, if followed, will keep you on that road. If you neglect to make the start, or stop before you arrive, no one will be to blame but YOU. This responsibility is yours. No excuse will save you from accepting the responsibility if you fail or refuse to demand riches of Life, because the acceptance calls for one thing—incidentally, the only thing you can control--and that is a STATE OF MIND. A state of mind is something that one assumes. It cannot be purchased; it must be created.

Fear of poverty is a state of mind, nothing else! But it is strong enough to destroy your chances of achievement, a truth that became painfully evident during the great depression and that could be realized again in the most recent recession. This fear paralyzes reason, destroys imagination, kills off self-reliance, undermines enthusiasm, discourages initiative, leads to uncertainty of purpose, encourages procrastination, wipes out enthusiasm, and makes self-control impossible. It takes the charm from personality, destroys accurate thinking, and diverts concentration of effort; it masters persistence, turns will-power into nothingness, destroys ambition, clouds the memory, and invites failure in every conceivable form. It kills love and assassinates the finer emotions of the heart, discourages friendship and invites disaster in a hundred forms, leads to sleeplessness, misery, and unhappiness—and all this, despite the fact that we live in a world of abundance, of everything the heart could desire, with nothing standing between us and our desires, except for lack of a definite purpose.

The Fear of Poverty is, without doubt, the most destructive of the six basic fears. It has been placed at the head of the list, because it is the most difficult to master. Considerable courage is required to face the origin of this fear, and still greater courage to accept the truth after facing it. The fear of poverty grew out of our inherited tendency to PREY ON OTHERS, ECONOMICALLY. Nearly all animals are motivated by instinct, but their capacity to "think" is limited, therefore, they prey on one another physically. Humans, with a superior sense of intuition, with the capacity to think and to reason, do not *eat* other people; we get more satisfaction out of devouring them FINANCIALLY. Humans are so greedy that we've had to pass every conceivable law to safeguard people against each other.

Of all periods in history, this one seems to be one of outstanding money-madness. People are considered less than the dust of the earth, unless they have money, and NO MATTER HOW THEY ACQUIRED IT, they have been permitted to live above the law, rule in politics, dominate in business, and the whole world bows in respect. Nothing brings more suffering and humility than POVERTY! Only those who have experienced poverty understand the full meaning of this.

It is no wonder we *fear* poverty. Through a long line of inherited experiences, we learned, for sure, that some people cannot be trusted, where matters of money and earthly possessions are concerned. This is a rather stinging indictment, the worst part of it being that it is TRUE. Many marriages are motivated by the wealth possessed by one, or both of the contracting parties. It is no wonder, therefore, that the divorce courts are so busy. So eager are people to possess wealth that they will acquire it in whatever manner they can—through legal methods if possible—through other methods if necessary or expedient.

Self-analysis may reveal weaknesses that we don't like to acknowledge. This form of examination is essential to all who demand of Life more than mediocrity and poverty. Remember, as you check yourself point by point, that you are both the court and the jury, the prosecuting attorney and the attorney for the defense, and that you are the plaintiff and the defendant—also, that you are on trial. Face the facts squarely. Ask yourself definite questions and demand direct replies. When the examination is over, you will know more about yourself. If you don't think you can be an impartial judge in this self-examination, find someone who knows you well to serve as judge while you cross-examine yourself. You are after the truth. *Get it, no matter what cost, even though it may temporarily embarrass you!*

The majority of people, if asked what they fear most, would reply, "I fear nothing." The reply would be inaccurate, because few people realize that they are bound, handicapped, whipped spiritually and physically through some form of fear. So subtle and deeply seated is the emotion of fear that one may go through life burdened with it, never recognizing its presence. Only a courageous analysis will disclose the presence of this universal enemy. When you begin such an analysis, search deeply into your character. Here is a list of the symptoms for which you should look:

SYMPTOMS OF THE FEAR OF POVERTY

INDIFFERENCE: Commonly expressed as lack of ambition; willingness to tolerate poverty; acceptance of whatever compensation life may offer without protest; mental and physical laziness; lack of initiative, imagination, enthusiasm, and self-control.

INDECISION: The habit of permitting others to do your thinking. Staying "on the fence."

DOUBT: Generally expressed through excuses designed to cover up, explain away, or apologize for one's failures; sometimes expressed in the form of envy of those who are successful, or by criticizing them.

WORRY: Usually expressed by finding fault with others, a tendency to spend beyond one's income, neglect of personal appearance, scowling and frowning; excessive use alcohol, sometimes narcotics; nervousness, lack of poise, self-consciousness, and lack of self-reliance.

OVER-CAUTION: The habit of looking for the negative side of every circumstance, thinking and talking of possible failure instead of concentrating on the means of succeeding. Knowing all the roads to disaster, but never searching for the plans to avoid failure. Waiting for "the right time" to begin putting ideas and plans into action, until the waiting becomes a permanent habit. Remembering those who have failed, and forgetting those who have succeeded. Seeing the hole in the doughnut, but overlooking the doughnut. Pessimism, leading to indigestion, poor elimination, autointoxication, and bad disposition.

PROCRASTINATION: The habit of putting off until tomorrow what should have been done last year. Spending enough time creating excuses to have done the job. This symptom is closely related to over-caution, doubt, and worry. Refusal to accept responsibility when it can be avoided. Willingness to compromise rather than put up a stiff fight. Compromising with difficulties instead of harnessing and using them as stepping stones to advancement. Bargaining with Life for a penny, instead of demanding prosperity, opulence, riches, contentment, and happiness. Planning what to do IF AND WHEN OVERTAKEN BY FAILURE, INSTEAD OF BURNING ALL BRIDGES AND MAKING RETREAT IMPOSSIBLE. Weakness of, and often total lack of self-confidence, definiteness of purpose, self-control, initiative, enthusiasm, ambition, thrift, and sound reasoning ability. EXPECTING POVERTY INSTEAD OF DEMANDING WEALTH. Association with those who accept poverty instead of seeking the company of those who demand and receive wealth.

MONEY TALKS!

Some will ask, "Why did you write a book about money? Why measure wealth in dollars, alone?" Some will believe, and rightly so, that there are other forms of riches more desirable than money. Yes, there are riches that cannot be measured in terms of dollars, but there are millions of people who will say, "Give me all the money I need, and I will find everything else I want."

The major reason why I wrote this book on how to get money is that the world has recently passed through an experience that left millions of people paralyzed with the FEAR OF POVERTY. What this sort of fear does to a person was well described by Westbrook Pegler, in the New York World-Telegram:

Money is only clam shells or metal discs or scraps of paper, and there are treasures of the heart and soul which money cannot buy, but most people, being broke, are unable to keep this in mind and sustain their spirits. When a person is down and out and on the street, unable to get a job, something happens to the spirit that can be seen in the droop of the shoulders, the walk, and the gaze. Such people cannot escape a feeling of inferiority among people with regular employment, even though they may not be equals in character, intelligence, or ability.

The more fortunate feel a sense of superiority and regard the unemployed, perhaps unconsciously, as a casualty. They may borrow for a time, but not enough to carry on in their accustomed ways, and they cannot borrow very long. But borrowing in itself, when a person is borrowing merely to live, is a depressing experience, and the money lacks the power of earned money to revive one's spirits. Of course, none of this applies to bums or habitual ne'er-do-wells, but only to those of normal ambitions and self-respect.

THE FEAR OF CRITICISM

Just how we originally came by this fear, no one can state definitely, but one thing is certain, we have it in a highly developed form. Some believe that this fear made its appearance about the time that politics became a "profession." Others believe it can be traced to the age when women first began to concern themselves with "styles" in clothing. Being neither a humorist nor a prophet, I am inclined to attribute the basic fear of criticism to that part of our inherited nature that prompts us, not only to take away from goods and wares of others, but to justify it by CRITICIZING character. It is well known that a thief will criticize the person from whom he steals—that politicians seek office, not by displaying their own virtues and qualifications, but by attempting to smear their opponents.

The fear of criticism takes on many forms, the majority of which are petty and trivial. The astute manufacturers of clothing have not been slow to capitalize this basic fear of criticism, with which all mankind has been cursed. Every season, the styles change. Who establishes the styles? Certainly not the purchaser of clothing, but the manufacturers. Why do they change the styles so often? The answer is obvious. They change the styles to sell more clothes. For the same reason, the manufacturers of automobiles (with a few rare and very sensible exceptions) change styles of models every year or two. No one wants to drive an automobile that is not of the latest style, although the older model may actually be the better car.

We have been describing the manner in which people behave under the influence of fear of criticism as applied to the small and petty things of life. Let us now examine human behavior when this fear affects people in connection with the more important events of human relationship. Take, for example, practically any person who has reached the age of "mental maturity" (from 35 to 40 years of age, as a general average), and if you could read the secret thoughts of their mind, you would find a very decided disbelief in the religious stories and fables we were told as children.

Not often, however, will you find a person with the courage to openly state his belief on this subject. Most people will, if pressed far enough, tell a lie rather than admit that they do not believe the stories associated with that form of religion that held people in bondage prior to the age of scientific discovery and education. Why does the average person, even in this day of enlightenment, shy away from denying belief in the fables, which were the basis of most of the world's religions? The answer is, "because of the fear of criticism." Men and women have been burned at the stake for daring to express disbelief in ghosts. It is no wonder we have inherited a consciousness that makes us fear criticism. The time was, and not so far in the past, when criticism carried severe punishments; it still does in some countries.

The fear of criticism robs us of initiative, destroys our power of imagination, limits our individuality, takes away our self-reliance, and damages us in a hundred other ways. Parents often do their children irreparable injury by criticizing them. The mother of one of my childhood friends used to punish him with a switch almost daily, always completing the job with the statement, "You'll land in the penitentiary before you are twenty." He was sent to a reformatory at the age of seventeen.

Criticism is one thing, of which we have all received too much. Everyone has a stock of it that is handed out freely, whether called for or not. One's nearest relatives often are the worst offenders. It should be recognized as a crime (in reality it is a crime of the worst nature), for any parent to build inferiority complexes in the mind of a child, through unnecessary criticism. Employers who understand human nature, get the best out of their employees, not by criticism, but by constructive suggestion and positive recognition. Parents may accomplish the same results with their children. Criticism plants FEAR in the human heart, or resentment, but it will not build love or affection.

SYMPTOMS OF THE FEAR OF CRITICISM

The fear of criticism is almost as universal as the fear of poverty, and its effects are just as fatal to personal achievement, mainly because this fear destroys initiative and discourages the use of imagination. The major symptoms of fear of criticism are:

SELF-CONSCIOUSNESS: Generally expressed through nervousness, timidity in conversation, and in meeting strangers; awkward movement of the hands and limbs, shifting of the eyes.

LACK OF POISE: Expressed through lack of voice control, nervous-ness in the presence of others, poor posture of body, poor memory.

WEAK PERSONALITY: Lacking firmness of decision, personal charm, and ability to express definite opinions. Side-stepping issues instead of meeting them squarely. Agreeing with others without careful examination of their opinions.

INFERIORITY COMPLEX: Expressing self-approval by word of mouth and by actions, as a means of covering up a feeling of inferiority. Using "big words" to impress others, (often without knowing the real meaning of the words). Imitating others in dress, speech, and manners. Boasting of exaggerated or imaginary achievements. This sometimes gives a surface appearance of a feeling of superiority.

EXTRAVAGANCE: The habit of trying to "keep up with the Joneses," spending beyond one's income.

LACK OF INITIATIVE: Failure to embrace opportunities for self-advancement, fear to express opinions, lack of confidence in one's own ideas, giving evasive answers to questions asked by superiors, hesitancy of manner and speech, deceit in both words and deeds.

LACK OF AMBITION: Mental and physical laziness, lack of self-assertion, slowness in reaching decisions, easily influenced by others, the habit of criticizing others behind their backs and flat-tering them to their faces; accepting defeat without protest, quitting an undertaking when opposed by others, suspicious of other people without cause, lacking tact and speech, unwillingness to accept the blame for mistakes.

THE FEAR OF ILLNESS

This fear may be traced to both physical and social heredity. It is closely associated with the fear of Old Age and the fear of Death. For the most part, we fear illness because of the terrible pictures that have been planted in our minds of what may happen if death should overtake us. We also fear it because of the economic toll it can claim.

A reputable physician estimated that 75% of all people who visit physicians for professional service are suffering with hypochondria (imaginary illness). It has been shown, most convincingly, that the fear of disease often produces the physical symptoms of the disease feared. Powerful and mighty is the human mind! It builds or it destroys.

Playing on this common weakness of fear of illness, pharmaceutical companies have reaped fortunes. During the "flu" epidemic that broke out during the world war, the mayor of New York City took drastic steps to check the damage people were doing themselves through their inherent fear of illness. He called in the newspaper reporters and said to them, "I feel it necessary to ask you not to publish any *scare headlines* concerning the 'flu' epidemic. Unless you cooperate with me, we will have a situation we cannot control." The newspapers quit publishing stories about the flu, and within one month, the epidemic had been successfully checked.

Through a series of experiments conducted some years ago, it was proved that people can become ill by suggestion. We conducted this experiment by having three acquaintances visit the "victims," each of whom asked the question, "What ails you? You look terribly ill." The first questioner usually provoked a grin, and a nonchalant "Oh, nothing, I'm alright," from the victim. The second questioner usually was answered with the statement, "I don't know exactly, but I do feel badly." By the time the third questioner approached the victim, he was usually met with the frank admission that the victim was actually feeling ill.

There is overwhelming evidence that disease sometimes begins in the form of negative thought impulse. Such an impulse may be passed from one mind to another, by suggestion, or created by individuals in their own minds. A person who was blessed with more wisdom than this incident might indicate, once said, "When anyone asks me how I feel, I always want to answer by knocking them down." Doctors send patients into new climates for their health, because a change of "mental attitude" is necessary. The seed of fear of illness lives in every human mind. Worry, fear, discouragement, disappointment in love and business affairs, cause this seed to germinate and grow. The recent business environment has kept the doctors on the run, because every form of negative thinking can cause illness.

SYMPTOMS OF THE FEAR OF ILLNESS

The symptoms of this almost universal fear are:

AUTO-SUGGESTION: Negative self-suggestion by looking for, and expecting to find the symptoms of all kinds of disease. "Enjoying" imaginary illness and speaking of it as being real. The habit of trying all "fads" and "isms" recommended by others as having therapeutic value. Talking to others of operations, accidents and other forms of illness. Experimenting with diets, exercises, and weight loss systems without professional guidance.

HYPOCHONDRIA: The habit of talking of illness, concentrating the mind on disease, and expecting its appearance until a nervous break occurs. Nothing that comes in bottles can cure this condition. It is brought on by negative thinking and nothing but positive thought can affect a cure. Hypochondria, a medical term for imaginary disease, is said to do as much damage, as the disease itself. Most so-called cases of "nerves" come from imaginary illness.

EXERCISE: Fear of illness often interferes with proper physical exercise, and results in obesity, by causing one to avoid outdoor life.

SUSCEPTIBILITY: Fear of illness breaks down nature's body resistance, and creates a favorable condition for any form of disease.

POVERTY: The fear of illness is often related to the fear of Poverty, especially in the case of the hypochondriac, who constantly worries about the possibility of having to pay doctor's bills, hospital bills, etc. This type of person spends much time preparing for sickness, talking about death, saving money for cemetery lots, and burial expenses, etc.

SELF-CODDLING: The habit of making a bid for sympathy, using imaginary illness as the lure. People often resort to this trick to avoid work. The habit of feigning illness to cover plain laziness, or to serve as an excuse for lack of ambition.

INTEMPERANCE: The habit of using alcohol or narcotics to destroy pains such as headaches, neuralgia, etc., instead of eliminating the cause.

THE FEAR OF OLD AGE

In the basic fear of old age, people have two very sound reasons for apprehension—one growing out of distrust for others, who seek to capitalize on through inheritance, and the other arising from the terrible fear of the unknown. The possibility of illness, which is more common as people grow older, is also a contributing cause of this common fear of old age. Ego also enters into the cause of the fear of old age, as no one cherishes the thought of diminishing physical attraction. The most common cause of fear of old age is associated with the possibility of poverty. Poorhouse is not a pretty word. It throws a chill into the mind of every person who faces the possibility of having to spend their declining years in poverty.

Another contributing cause of the fear of old age, is the possibility of loss of freedom and independence, as old age may bring with it the loss of both physical and economic freedom.

SYMPTOMS OF THE FEAR OF OLD AGE

The three most common symptoms of this fear are:

1. The tendency to slow down and develop an inferiority complex at the age of mental maturity, around the age of forty, falsely believing one's self to be "slipping" because of age. (The truth is that our most useful years, mentally and spiritually, are between forty and sixty).
2. The habit of speaking apologetically as "being old" merely because one has reached the age of forty or fifty, instead of reversing the rule and expressing gratitude for having reached the age of wisdom and understanding.
3. The habit of killing off initiative, imagination, and self-reliance by falsely believing one's self too old to exercise these qualities. The habit of the man or woman of forty dressing with the aim of trying to appear much younger, and affecting mannerisms of youth, inspiring ridicule from friends and strangers.

THE FEAR OF DEATH

To some this is the cruelest of all the basic fears. The reason is obvious. The most common causes of the fear of death are ill-health, poverty, lack of appropriate occupation, disappointment over love, insanity, and religious fanaticism. The terrible pangs of fear associated with the thought of death, in the majority of cases, can be directly attributed to religious fanaticism. So-called "heathen" are less afraid of death than the more "civilized." For hundreds of millions of years we have been asking the still unanswered questions, where did I come from, and where am I going?

During the dark ages, the more cunning and crafty were not slow to offer the answer to these questions, FOR A PRICE. Witness, now, the major source of origin of the FEAR OF DEATH.

"Come into my tent, embrace my faith, accept my dogmas, and I will give you a ticket that will admit you straightaway into heaven when you die," cries a leader of sectarianism. "Remain out of my tent," says the same leader, "and may the devil take you and burn you throughout eternity."

ETERNITY is a long time. FIRE is a terrible thing. The thought of eternal punishment, with fire, not only causes us to fear death, it often causes us to lose reason. It destroys interest in life and makes happiness impossible. During my research, I read a book entitled *A Catalogue of the Gods* that listed the *30,000* gods man has worshiped through history. Think of it! Thirty thousand of them, represented by everything from a crawfish to a man. It is little wonder that we have become frightened at the approach of death.

While the religious leader may not be able to provide sure entry into heaven, nor, by lack of such provision, allow the unfortunate to descend into hell, the possibility of the latter seems so terrible that the very thought of it lays hold of the imagination in such a realistic way that it paralyzes reason, and sets up the fear of death.

In truth, NO ONE KNOWS, and no one has ever known, what heaven or hell is like, nor does any one know if either place actually exists. This very lack of positive knowledge opens the door of the human mind to the charlatan so he may enter and control that mind with his stock of deceit and various brands of fraud and trickery. The fear of DEATH is not as common now as it was during the age when there were no great colleges and universities. People of science have turned the spotlight of truth on the world, and this truth is rapidly freeing men and women from this terrible fear of DEATH. The young people who attend the colleges and universities are not easily impressed by "fire" and "brimstone." Through the aid of biology, astronomy, geology, and other related sciences, the fears of the dark ages, which gripped minds and destroyed their reason, have been dispelled.

Insane asylums are filled with people who have gone mad, because of the FEAR OF DEATH. This fear is useless. Death will come, no matter what anyone may think about it. Accept it as a necessity, and pass the thought out of your mind. It must be a necessity, or it would not come to all. Perhaps it is not as bad as it has been pictured. The entire world is made up of only two things, ENERGY and MATTER. In elementary physics, we learn that neither matter nor energy (the only two realities known to man) can be created or destroyed. Both matter and energy can be transformed, but neither can be destroyed.

Life is energy, if it is anything. If neither energy nor matter can be destroyed, of course life cannot be destroyed. Life, like other forms of energy, may be passed through various processes of transition, or change, but it cannot be destroyed. Death is mere transition. If death is not mere change, or transition, then nothing comes after death except a long, eternal, peaceful sleep, and sleep is nothing to be feared. Thus, you can wipe out, forever, the fear of Death.

SYMPTOMS OF THE FEAR OF DEATH

The general symptom of this fear is the habit of THINKING about dying instead of making the most of LIFE, due, generally, to lack of purpose, or lack of a suitable occupation. This fear is more prevalent among the aged, but sometimes the more youthful are victims of it. The greatest of all remedies for the fear of death is a BURNING DESIRE FOR ACHIEVEMENT, backed by useful service to others. Busy people seldom have time to think about dying. They find life too thrilling to worry about death. Sometimes the fear of death is closely associated with the Fear of Poverty, where one's death would leave loved ones poverty-stricken. In other cases, the fear of death is caused by illness and the breaking down of the physical body.

WORRY

Worry is a state of mind based on fear. It works slowly, but persistently. It is insidious and subtle. Step by step it "digs itself in" until it paralyzes the ability to reason and destroys self-confidence and initiative. Worry is a form of sustained fear caused by indecision. Therefore, it is a state of mind that can be controlled.

An unsettled mind is helpless. Indecision makes an unsettled mind. Most individuals lack the willpower to reach decisions promptly, and to stand by them after they have been made, even during normal business conditions. During periods of economic unrest (such as the world recently experienced), the individual is handicapped. Standing alone, with the inherent nature to be slow at reaching decisions, these people are influenced by the indecision of others around them who have created a state of "mass indecision."

During the great depression, the whole atmosphere, all over the world, was filled with "Fearenza" and "Worryitis," the two mental disease germs that began to spread themselves after the Wall Street frenzy in 1929. There is only one known antidote for these germs; it is the habit of prompt and firm DECISION. Moreover, it is an antidote which every individual must administer themselves. We do not worry over conditions, once we have reached a decision to follow a definite line of action. I once interviewed a man who was to be electrocuted two hours later. The condemned man was the calmest of the eight men who were in the death-cell with him. His calmness prompted me to ask him how it felt to know that he was going into eternity in a short while. With a smile of confidence on his face, he said, "It feels fine. Just think, brother, my troubles will soon be over. I have had nothing but trouble all my life. It has been a hardship to get food and clothing. Soon I will not need these things. I have felt fine ever since I learned FOR CERTAIN that I will die. I made up my mind then, to accept my fate in good spirit."

As he spoke, he devoured a dinner of proportions sufficient for three men, eating every mouthful of the food brought to him, and apparently enjoying it as much as if no disaster awaited him. DECISION gave this man resignation to his fate! Decision can also prevent one's acceptance of undesired circumstances.

The six basic fears become translated into a state of worry, through indecision. Relieve yourself, forever of the fear of death, by reaching a decision to accept death as an inescapable event. Whip the fear of poverty by reaching a decision to get along with whatever wealth you can accumulate WITHOUT WORRY. Put your foot down on the fear of criticism by reaching a decision NOT TO WORRY about what other people think, do, or say. Eliminate the fear of old age by reaching a decision to accept it, not as a handicap, but as a great blessing which carries with it wisdom, self-control, and understanding not known to youth. Acquit yourself of the fear of ill health by the decision to forget symptoms. Kill the habit of worry, in all its forms, by reaching a general, blanket decision that nothing life has to offer is worth the price of worry. With this decision will come poise, peace of mind, and calmness of thought that will bring happiness.

People whose minds are filled with fear not only destroy their chances of intelligent action, but transmit these destructive vibrations to the minds of all who come into contact with them. Even a dog or a horse knows when its master lacks courage; moreover, a dog or a horse will pick up the vibrations of fear thrown off by its master, and behave accordingly. Lower down the line of intelligence in the animal kingdom, one finds this same capacity to pick up the vibrations of fear. A honey-bee immediately senses fear in the mind of a person. For reasons unknown, a bee will sting the person whose mind is releasing vibrations of fear, much more readily than it will the person whose mind registers no fear.

The vibrations of fear pass from one mind to another just as quickly and as surely as the sound of the human voice passes from the broadcasting station to the receiving set of a radio--and BY THE SELF-SAME MEDIUM.

Mental telepathy is a reality. Thoughts pass from one mind to another, voluntarily, whether or not this is recognized by either the person releasing the thoughts, or the persons who pick up those thoughts. The person who gives expression, by word of mouth, to negative or destructive thoughts is practically certain to experience the results of those words in the form of a destructive "kick-back." The release of destructive thought impulses, alone, without the aid of words, produces also a "kickback" in many ways. First, and perhaps most important to be remembered, the person who releases thoughts of a destructive nature, must suffer damage of the breaking down of creative imagination. Second, the presence in the mind of any destructive emotion develops a negative personality that repels people, and often converts them into antagonists. The third source of damage to the person who entertains or releases negative thoughts, lies in this significant fact--these thought-impulses are not only damaging to others, but they IMBED THEMSELVES IN THE SUBCONSCIOUS MIND OF THE PERSON RELEASING THEM, and become a part of his character.

One is never through with a thought, merely by releasing it. When a thought is released, it spreads in every direction, through the medium of the ether, but it also plants itself *permanently* in the subconscious mind of *the person releasing it.*

Your business in life is, presumably to achieve success. To be successful, you must find peace of mind, acquire the material needs of life, and above all, attain HAPPINESS. All of these evidences of success begin in the form of thought impulses. You can control your own mind; you have the power to feed it whatever thought impulses you choose. With this privilege comes the responsibility of using it constructively. You are the master of your own earthly destiny just as surely as you have the power to control your own thoughts. You may influence, direct, and eventually control your own environment, making your life what you want it to be— or, you may neglect to exercise the privilege which is yours, to make your life to order, thus casting yourself into the broad sea of "Circumstance" where you will be tossed around on the waves of the ocean.

THE DEVIL'S WORKSHOP

THE SEVENTH BASIC EVIL

In addition to the Six Basic Fears, there is another evil people suffer from. It constitutes a rich soil in which the seeds of failure grow abundantly. It is so subtle that its presence often is not detected. This affliction cannot properly be classified as a fear. IT IS MORE DEEPLY SEATED AND MORE OFTEN FATAL THAN ALL OF THE FEARS. For want of a better name, let us call this evil SUSCEPTIBILITY TO NEGATIVE INFLUENCES.

People who accumulate great wealth always protect themselves against this evil! The poverty stricken never do! Those who succeed in any calling must prepare their minds to resist the evil. If you are reading this philosophy to accumulate wealth, you should examine yourself very carefully, to determine whether you are susceptible to negative influences. If you neglect this self-analysis, you will forfeit your right to attain the object of your desires. Make the analysis searching. After you read the questions prepared for this self-analysis, hold yourself to a strict accounting in your answers. Go at the task as carefully as you would search for any other enemy you knew to be awaiting you in ambush, and deal with your own faults as you would a more tangible enemy.

You can easily protect yourself against highway robbers, because the law provides organized cooperation for your benefit, but the "seventh basic evil" is more difficult to master, because it strikes when you are not aware of its presence, when you are asleep and while you are awake. Moreover, its weapon is intangible, because it consists of merely a STATE OF MIND. This evil is also dangerous because it strikes in as many different forms as there are human experiences. Sometimes it enters the mind through the well-meant words of relatives. At other times, it bores from within, through one's own mental attitude. Always it is as deadly as poison, even though it may not kill as quickly.

PROTECT YOURSELF AGAINST NEGATIVE INFLUENCES

To protect yourself against negative influences, whether of your own making, or the result of negative people around you, recognize that you have a WILL-POWER, and put it into constant use, until it builds a wall of immunity against negative influences in your own mind. Recognize that you, and every other human being, are, by nature, lazy, indifferent, and susceptible to all suggestions that harmonize with your weaknesses.

Recognize that you are, by nature, susceptible to all the basic fears, and set up habits that will counteract these fears. Recognize that negative influences often work through your subconscious mind, making them difficult to detect. Keep your mind closed against all people who depress or discourage you in any way. Clean out your medicine chest, throw away all pill bottles, and stop pandering to colds, aches, pains, and imaginary illness.

Deliberately seek the company of people who influence you to THINK AND ACT FOR YOURSELF. Do not EXPECT troubles as they have a tendency not to disappoint. *Without doubt, the most common weakness of all human beings is the habit of leaving their minds open to the negative influence of other people.* This weakness is all the more damaging, because most people do not recognize that they are cursed by it, and many who acknowledge it, neglect or refuse to correct it until it becomes an uncontrollable part of their daily habits.

To aid those who wish to see themselves as they really are, the following list of questions has been prepared. Read the questions and state your answers aloud, so you can hear your own voice. This will make it easier for you to be truthful with yourself.

SELF-ANALYSIS TEST QUESTIONS

1. Do you complain often of feeling bad, and if so, what is the cause?

   _____

2. Do you find fault with other people at the slightest provocation?

   _____

3. Do you frequently make mistakes in your work, and if so, why?

   _____

4. Are you sarcastic and offensive in your conversation?

   _____

5. Do you deliberately avoid the association of anyone, and if so, why?

   _____

6. Do you suffer frequently with indigestion? If so, what is the cause?

_____

7. Does life seem futile and the future hopeless to you? If so, why?

_____

8. Do you like your occupation? If not, why not?

_____

9. Do you often feel self-pity, and if so why?

_____

10. Are you envious of those who are more successful than you?

_____

11. Do you devote more time to thinking of SUCCESS, or of FAILURE?

_____

12. Are you gaining or losing self-confidence as you grow older?

_____

13. Do you learn something of value from all mistakes? Give examples.

_____

14. Are you permitting some relative or acquaintance to worry you? If so, why?

_____

15. Are you sometimes "in the clouds" and at other times in the depths of despondency?

_____

16. Who has the most inspiring influence on you? What is the cause?

_____

17. Do you tolerate negative or discouraging influences that you can avoid?

_____

18. Are you careless of your personal appearance? If so, when and why?

_____

19. Have you learned how to "drown your troubles" by being too busy to be annoyed by them?

_____

20. Would you call yourself a spineless weakling if you allowed others to do your thinking for you?

_____

21. How many preventable disturbances annoy you, and why do you tolerate them?

_____

22. Do you resort to liquor, narcotics, or cigarettes to "quiet your nerves"? If so, why do you not try will-power instead?

_____

23. Does anyone "nag" you, and if so, for what reason?

_____

24. Do you have a DEFINITE MAJOR PURPOSE, and if so, what is it, and what plan do you have for achieving it?

_____

25. Do you suffer from any of the Five Basic Fears? If so, which ones?

_____

26. Do you have a method by which you can shield yourself against the negative influence of others?

_____

27. Do you make deliberate use of auto-suggestion to make your mind positive?

_____

28. Which do you value most, your material possessions, or the privilege of controlling your own thoughts?

_____

29. Are you easily influenced by others, against your own judgment?

_____

30. Has today added anything of value to your stock of knowledge or state of mind?

31. Do you face squarely the circumstances that make you unhappy, or sidestep the responsibility?

32. Do you analyze all mistakes and failures and try to profit by them, or do you take the attitude that this is not your duty?

33. Can you name three of your most damaging weaknesses? What are you doing to correct them?

34. Do you encourage other people to bring their worries to you for sympathy?

35. Do you choose, from your daily experiences, lessons or influences which aid in your personal advancement?

36. Does your presence have a negative influence on other people as a rule?

37. What habits of other people annoy you most?

38. Do you form your own opinions or permit yourself to be influenced by other people?

39. Have you learned how to create a mental state of mind with which you can shield yourself against all discouraging influences?

40. Does your occupation inspire you with faith and hope?

41. Are you conscious of possessing spiritual forces of sufficient power to enable you to keep your mind free from all forms of FEAR?

42. Does your religion help you to keep your own mind positive?

_____

43. Do you feel it your duty to share other people's worries? If so, why?

_____

44. If you believe that "birds of a feather flock together," what have you learned about yourself by studying the friends you attract?

_____

45. What connection, if any, do you see between the people with whom you associate most closely, and any unhappiness you may experience?

_____

46. Is it possible that some person you consider to be a friend is, in reality, working against you because of the negative influence they bring to your mind?

_____

47. By what rules do you judge who is helpful and who is damaging to you?

_____

48. Are your intimate associates mentally superior or inferior to you?

_____

49. How much time out of every 24 hours do you devote to:
   a. your occupation -
   b. sleep -
   c. play and relaxation -
   d. acquiring useful knowledge -
   e. plain waste –

Who among your acquaintances,
   f. encourages you most -
   g. inspires you most -
   h. cautions you most -
   i. discourages you most -

50. What is your greatest worry? Why do you tolerate it?

_____

51. When others offer you free, unsolicited advice, do you accept it without question, or analyze their motive?

_____

52. What, above all else, do you most DESIRE? Do you intend to acquire it? Are you willing to subordinate all other desires for this one? How much time daily do you devote to acquiring it?

_____

53. Do you change your mind often? If so, why?

_____

54. Do you usually finish everything you begin?

_____

55. Are you easily impressed by other people's business or professional titles, college degrees, or wealth?

_____

56. Are you easily influenced by what other people think or say of you?

_____

57. Do you cater to people because of their social or financial status?

_____

58. Whom do you believe to be the greatest person living? In what respect is this person superior to yourself?

_____

If you have answered all these questions truthfully, you know more about yourself than the majority of people. Study the questions carefully, come back to them once each week for several months, and be astounded at the amount of additional knowledge of great value to yourself, you will have gained by the simple method of answering the questions truthfully. If you are not certain of the answers to some of the questions, seek the counsel of those who know you well, especially those who have no motive in flattering you, and see yourself through their eyes. The experience will be astonishing.

u have ABSOLUTE CONTROL over only one thing, and that is your thoughts. This is the most significant and inspiring of all facts known to man! It reflects our Divine nature. This Divine prerogative is the sole means by which you can control your own destiny. If you fail to control your own mind, you will control nothing else. If you must be careless with your possessions, let it be in connection with material things. *Your mind is your spiritual estate!* Protect and use it with the care to which Divine Royalty is entitled. You were given a WILL-POWER for this purpose.

Unfortunately, there is no legal protection against those who, either by design or ignorance, poison the minds of others by negative suggestion. This form of destruction should be punishable by heavy legal penalties, because it can and often does destroy one's chances of acquiring the material things that are protected by law. People with negative minds tried to convince Thomas A. Edison that he could not build a machine that would record and reproduce the human voice, "because" they said, "no one else had ever produced such a machine." Edison did not believe them. He knew that the mind could produce ANYTHING IT COULD CONCEIVE AND BELIEVE, and that knowledge was the thing that lifted the great Edison above the common herd.

People with negative minds told F. W. Woolworth, he would go "broke" trying to run a store on five and ten cent sales. He did not believe them. He knew that he could do anything, within reason, if he backed his plans with faith. Exercising his right to keep other people's negative suggestions out of his mind, he piled up a fortune of tremendous wealth. People with negative minds told George Washington he could not hope to win against the vastly superior forces of the British, but he exercised his Divine right to BELIEVE. As a result, this book was published under the protection of the Stars and Stripes, while the name of Lord Cornwallis has been all but forgotten.

Doubting Thomases scoffed scornfully when Henry Ford tried out his first crudely built automobile on the streets of Detroit. Some said the thing never would become practical. Others said no one would pay money for such a contraption. FORD SAID, "I'LL BELT THE EARTH WITH DEPENDABLE MOTOR CARS," AND HE DID! His decision to trust his own judgment piled up a fortune far greater than the next five generations of his descendents can squander. For the benefit of those seeking vast riches, let it be remembered that the sole difference between Henry Ford and a majority of the nearly three hundred thousand people who work for Ford, is this—FORD HAD A MIND AND CONTROLLED IT, THE OTHERS HAVE MINDS WHICH THEY DO NOT TRY TO CONTROL.

Henry Ford has been repeatedly mentioned, because he was an astounding example of what a person with a mind of his own, and a will to control it, can accomplish. His record knocks the foundation from under that time-worn excuse, "I never had a chance." Ford never had a chance either, but he CREATED AN OPPORTUNITY AND BACKED IT WITH PERSISTENCE UNTIL IT MADE HIM RICHER THAN CROESUS.

Mind control is the result of self-discipline and habit. You either control your mind or it controls you. There is no half-way compromise. The most practical of all methods for controlling the mind is the habit of keeping it busy with a definite purpose, backed by a definite plan. Study the record of any one who achieves noteworthy success, and you will observe that they control their own mind, moreover, they exercise that control and direct it toward the attainment of definite goals. Without this control, success is not possible.

FAMOUS EXCUSES By Old Man IF

People who do not succeed have one distinguishing trait in common. They know *all the reasons for failure*, and have what they believe to be air-tight alibis to explain away their own lack of achievement. Some of these excuses are clever, and a few of them are justifiable by the facts. But excuses cannot be used for money. The world wants to know only one thing: HAVE YOU ACHIEVED SUCCESS?

A character analyst compiled a list of the most commonly used excuses. As you read the list, examine yourself carefully, and determine how many of these excuses, if any, are your own property. Remember, too, the philosophy presented in this book makes every one of these excuses obsolete.

IF I didn't have a family to support. . .

IF I had enough "pull" . . .

IF I had money . . .

IF I had a good education . . .

IF I could get a job . . .

IF I had good health . . .

IF I only had time . . .

IF times were better . . .

IF other people understood me . . .

IF conditions around me were only different . . .

IF I could live my life over again . . .

IF I did not fear what "THEY" would say . . .

IF I had been given a chance . . .

IF I now had a chance . . .

IF other people didn't "have it in for me" . . .

IF nothing happens to stop me . . .

IF I were only younger . . .

IF I could only do what I want . . .

IF I had been born rich . . .

IF I could meet "the right people" . . .

IF I had the talent that some people have . . .

IF I dared assert myself . . .

IF I only had embraced past opportunities . . .

IF people didn't get on my nerves . . .

IF I didn't have to raise my children . . .

IF I could save some money . . .

IF the boss only appreciated me . . .

IF I only had somebody to help me . . .

IF my family understood me . . .

IF I lived in a big city . . .

IF I could just get started . . .

IF I were only free . . .

IF I had the personality of some people . . .

IF I were not so fat . . .

IF my talents were known .. •

IF I could just get a "break" . . .

IF I could only get out of debt . . .

IF I hadn't failed . . .

IF I only knew how . . .

IF everybody didn't oppose me . . .

IF I didn't have so many worries . . .

IF I could marry the right person . . .

IF people weren't so dumb . . .

IF my family were not so extravagant . . .

IF I were sure of myself . . .

IF luck were not against me . . .

IF I had not been born under the wrong star . . .

IF it were not true that "what is to be will be" . . .

IF I did not have to work so hard . . .

IF I hadn't lost my money . . .

IF I lived in a different neighborhood . . .

IF I didn't have a "past" . . .

IF I only had a business of my own . . .

IF other people would only listen to me . . .

IF...and this is the greatest of them all... I had the courage to see myself as I really am, I would *find out what is wrong with me*, and correct it, then I might have a chance to profit by my mistakes and learn something from the experience of others, for I know that there is something WRONG with me, or I would now be where *I WOULD HAVE BEEN IF* I had spent more time analyzing my weaknesses, and less time creating excuses to cover them.

Creating excuses to explain away failure is a national pastime. The habit is as old as the human race, and is *fatal to success!* Why do people cling to their pet excuses? The answer is obvious. They defend their excuses because THEY CREATE them! A person's excuse is the child of his own imagination. It is human nature to defend one's own brain-child. Creating excuses is a deeply rooted habit. Habits are difficult to break, especially when they provide justification for something we do. Plato had this truth in mind when he said, "The first and best victory is to conquer self. To be conquered by self is, of all things, the most shameful and vile."

Another philosopher had the same thought in mind when he said, "It was a great surprise to me when I discovered that most of the ugliness I saw in others, was only a reflection of my own nature."

"It has always been a mystery to me," said Elbert Hubbard, "why people spend so much time deliberately fooling themselves by creating excuses to cover their weaknesses. If used differently, this same time would be sufficient to cure the weakness, and no excuses would be needed."

In parting, I would remind you that "life is a checkerboard, and the player opposite you is TIME. If you hesitate before moving, or neglect to move promptly, your men will be wiped off the board by TIME. You are playing against a partner who will not tolerate INDECISION!"

Previously you may have had a logical excuse for not having forced Life to come through with whatever you asked, but that alibi is now obsolete, because you are in possession of the Master Key that unlocks the door to Life's bountiful riches. The Master Key is intangible, but it is powerful! It is the privilege of creating, *in your own mind*, a BURNING DESIRE for a defined form of wealth. There is no penalty for the use of the Key, but there is a price you must pay if you do not use it. The price is FAILURE. There is a reward of stupendous proportions if you put the Key to use. It is the satisfaction that comes to all who *conquer self and force Life to pay whatever is asked.*

The reward is worthy of your effort. Will you make the start and be convinced?

Made in the USA
Lexington, KY
13 April 2015